Haynes

Coarse Fishing Manual

The step-by-step guide

Kevin Green

BEST BAITS • EXPERT RIGS • TOP TIPS TO HELP YOU CATCH MORE FISH

CONTENTS

Introduction and acknowledgements   **6**

1   Know your species   8

Carp	10
Barbel	12
Dace	12
Pike	13
Bream	14
Perch	15
Tench	16
Crucian carp	17
Gudgeon	17
Chub	18
Rudd	18
Roach	19
Eel	19
Catfish	20
Zander	21
Grayling	21

2   Float fishing   22

Essential kit for stillwater float fishing	24
Waggler fishing kit essential extras	32
The four golden rules of waggler fishing	34
Setting up a waggler rig	36
Plumbing the depth	38
Three essential waggler rigs	40
Casting a float	41
Feeding on the float	42
Striking and landing fish	44
Waggler float fishing tips	46
The pellet waggler	48
Learning the stick float	51
Combating fast water	53
Easily hooked	54
Baiting your hook	56

Haynes

Coarse
Fishing
Manual

First published in September 2011
Reprinted June 2012 and February 2013
Reprinted in paperback June 2016

British Library Cataloguing in Publication Data
A catalogue record for this book is available from the British Library

ISBN 978 1 78521 090 7

Library of Congress control no. 2016937304

Published by Haynes Publishing,
Sparkford, Yeovil, Somerset BA22 7JJ, UK
Tel: 01963 440635
Int. tel: +44 1963 440635
Website: www.haynes.co.uk

Haynes North America Inc.
861 Lawrence Drive, Newbury Park,
California 91320, USA

Printed in the USA by Odcombe Press LP,
1299 Bridgestone Parkway, La Vergne, TN 37086

Credits

Author:	**Kevin Green**
Project manager:	**Louise McIntyre**
Copy editor:	**Ian Heath**
Page design:	**James Robertson**
Photography:	**Mick Rouse** **Lloyd Rogers** **Paul Garner** **Brian Skoyles** **Kevin Green**
Illustrations:	**David Batten**

3 Swimfeeder fishing — 60

Essential kit for swimfeeder fishing	64
Kit extras that'll get you geared up	68
The open-end feeder explained	70
Making groundbait	72
The block-end feeder explained	74
The flatbed method feeder explained	76
The method feeder explained	79
The time-bomb river feeder explained	82
The pellet feeder explained	86
How to cast a feeder	94
Setting up your seat box or chair	96
Legering	98
Hookbaits for feeders	102
Get the best from your feeder fishing	105

5 Carp fishing — 140

Essential kit for carping	142
Laying out your carp kit	146
Understanding carp rig materials	148
Tying a hooklink	152
How to make a coated braid hooklink	154
Putting together a lead clip	156
Putting together a running leger clip	158
Boilies – cutting through the confusion	160
Hookbaits to catch carp	162
Spot-on casting	165
Spodding – the accurate way to bait up	168
Landing, unhooking, weighing and releasing a carp	171

4 Pole fishing — 106

Essential kit for pole fishing	108
Elasticating	112
Shotting up a pole rig	118
Know your floats	120
Making a pole rig	122
Balancing your tackle	126
Setting up for pole fishing	128
Plumbing for pole fishing	132
The importance of feeding	134
Catching fish on the pole	138

6 Pike fishing — 174

Understanding pike fishing	176
Essential kit for piking	178
Tying a wire trace	181
Setting up a float rig	186
Mounting deadbaits and a long-range leger rig	188
Looking after your pike	190

Glossary — 192

Introduction

Welcome to coarse fishing. You're joining the ranks of one of the biggest participation sports in the world, and the good news is that there's never been a better time to start.

Fishing has undergone a massive transformation in the last decade, with huge advances in tackle, bait and fisheries. It's not only cheaper to take up fishing today, it's also easier than ever to learn the skills and to catch fish.

So where do you start? How do you begin to understand the techniques, the baits at your disposal and the fish you'll soon be catching?

To best understand this pastime it makes sense if we start by giving you a brief overview of coarse fishing basics, namely the different ways to catch fish and the main types of venue. Let's start with a look at the places where coarse fishing takes place.

Where to fish

Coarse fishing takes place in freshwater lakes, ponds, reservoirs, canals and rivers. The origin of the term 'coarse' fishing stems from the fact that you're aiming to catch fish other than salmon or trout, which are considered game fish.

In centuries past coarse fish were seen as being inferior to the grander game species that were the preserve of the aristocracy, but as time has passed it's coarse fishing that has become the more popular, and the growth of man-made commercial fisheries has further enhanced its dominance.

Just in case you get confused by terminology, it's worth clarifying from the start that there's no difference between the words 'fishing' and 'angling' – they mean the same thing. If you go fishing you go angling; if you're a fisherman you're also an angler.

Whatever you call it, the fact is that wherever you live there are good coarse fisheries on your doorstep – learn how to fish them and you've got a great hobby for life.

The basic styles of fishing

To make it easier to understand the different disciplines of coarse fishing we've split these into five basic approaches that encapsulate most of the ways to catch fish. Each of these styles – float, swimfeeder, pole, carp and pike – has a chapter dedicated to it so that you can easily learn everything you need to know in order to get started and to rapidly improve your fishing.

1 Float fishing

This is the traditional style of fishing that most people know. Put simply it's the use of a rod, reel, line and a float which signals when a fish has picked up your bait by lifting or going under the water.

There's a wide choice of tackle and floats available, and depending on what you choose you can use this style of fishing in any type of fishery, from the smallest farm pond to the fastest-flowing river.

2 Swimfeeder fishing

This is another style of angling with a rod and line, the big difference being that you don't use a float to register a bite from a fish. Instead you rely on the movement of the fine rod tip to tell you a fish is munching your bait.

The other key difference with this style, compared to float fishing, is that you attach a heavy tube or cage to your line called a 'swimfeeder'. Not only does this gadget help you cast your baited hook into the water, it's also loaded with extra bait to attract fish towards your hook. Once in the water this bait is washed out of the feeder to accurately position an extra meal alongside the bait on your hook. This increases the attractiveness of the area and makes it more likely that a hungry fish will investigate.

3 Pole fishing

In some ways pole fishing is the oldest of all types of angling – when a piece of string and a bent pin was first tied to a stick it was a type of pole fishing! Thankfully things have developed a long way since then and pole fishing has undergone a dramatic transformation in recent decades.

With no reel and line attached to a pole like it is with a rod, a pole is fitted with thick elastic running through the top few sections. A length of line holding a small float and the hook is attached directly to the elastic. When a fish is hooked the elastic stretches like a bungee to sap its strength and help bring it to the net.

4 Specialist carp fishing

The biggest growth area in coarse angling in the last 20 years has been the pursuit of large, specimen carp. This species of fish grows big, they fight like tigers, and a whole specialist style of fishing has developed to make catching them easier. A new class of baits and high-tech items of tackle have been formulated, and it's now common to see lakes surrounded by small tents (known as 'bivvies') as specialist carp anglers pursue big fish night and day.

Once considered a complicated fishing technique that could only be considered after many years' pursuit of smaller species, the growth in ready-made baits and off-the-shelf tackle has made specimen carp fishing far easier to learn.

5 Pike fishing

The vast majority of freshwater species are not actively carnivorous, but there are a few that strike fear into their smaller brethren. King of such predatory fish is the pike, a lean, mean, killing machine that's top of the food chain and, thanks to a fearsome set of fangs, can only be safely tackled by the use of specially designed tackle. We'll look at how you catch them in detail in the final chapter of this book.

And there you have it. Coarse fishing has been basically explained and the five main ways to catch fish have been identified. In the rest of this manual we'll take you though each of these fishing disciplines one by one, and by the time you get to the last page you'll have all the information you need to catch fish like an expert.

Let's get started, then – there's lots of fish out there waiting to be caught, and the sooner you know how to do it the better!

Acknowledgements

Special thanks go to Mick Rouse, Lloyd Rogers, Paul Garner and *Improve Your Coarse Fishing* for supplying excellent pictures. Thanks also to my colleagues on *IYCF* who gathered some of the original material.

In addition I'd like to acknowledge the many fisheries that have helped me over the years, and especially Lemington Lakes (www.lemingtonlakes. co.uk), who gave me full access to their superb waters for some of the pictures used in this guide. It's a great fishery.

Thanks also go to my wife Jo, and my young son Reuben who put up with dad disappearing on a regular basis as he went in search of words, fish or both.

Finally, this book is dedicated to my mum and dad. They fuelled and financed my early love of fishing and encouraged me every step of the way. They can never fully know how much I value their amazing support.

Kevin Green
March 2011

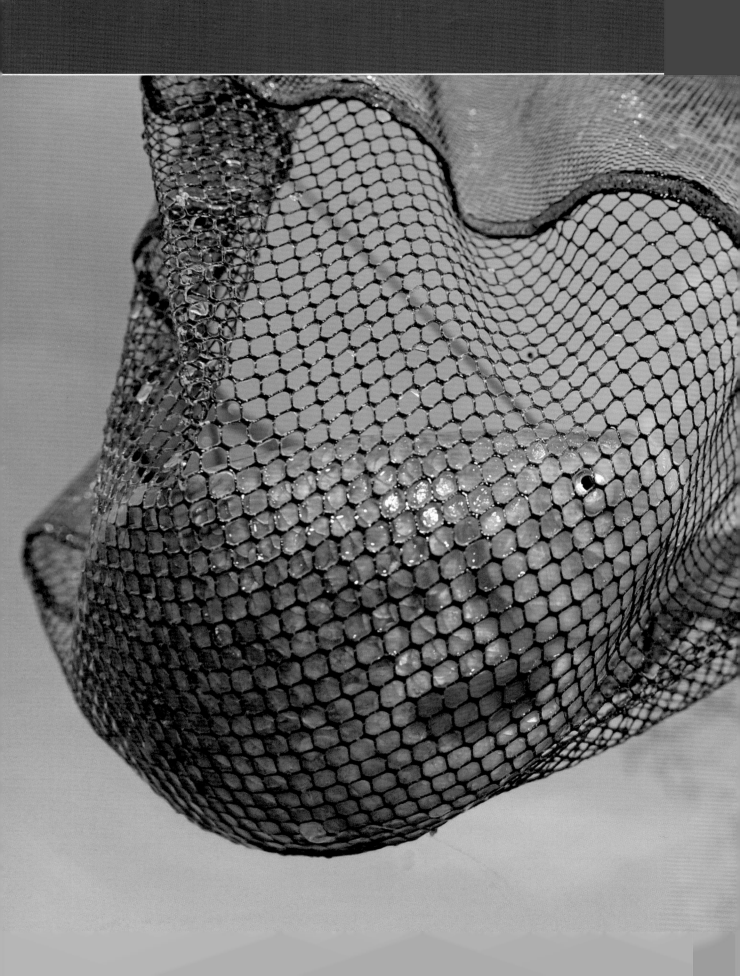

KNOW YOUR SPECIES

Carp 10

Barbel 12

Dace 12

Pike 13

Bream 14

Perch 15

Tench 16

Crucian carp 17

Gudgeon 17

Chub 18

Rudd 18

Roach 19

Eel 19

Catfish 20

Zander 21

Grayling 21

Knowing what species you're fishing for or what you've caught is vital information.

There are lots of different species of coarse fish living in freshwater lakes, canals and rivers, so it's essential that you can recognise your target fish and understand the key behaviour patterns they display.

One of the most basic mistakes that newcomers to fishing can make is to treat all fish as the same – they're most definitely not! In the same way that a cat and a dog differ wildly in their traits, so different types of fish display species-specific behaviours, and you'll need to remember these 'personalities' if you want to catch a certain type of fish.

The better you understand how a specific species behaves and what characteristics distinguish it from the others, the more you'll be able to shape your tactics to catch what you want.

Here's an overview of what sets different species of fish apart.

Carp

One of the biggest and most powerful freshwater species, several slightly different variants of carp exist that display different scale patterns to give them a unique character.

Below: Small scales cover a common carp.

Carp are now the number one coarse fish species in the world, so a large part of this book is dedicated to showing you how to catch them in different ways. The float, swimfeeder and pole chapters deal with methods of catching the small to medium-sized fish that now dominate many still waters, while in Chapter 5 we look at specialist methods that have been purpose-designed to catch very big, specimen carp.

Left: Randomly scattered large scales are found on a mirror carp.

General characteristics

- Usually found in stillwater lakes and ponds but can flourish in rivers.
- Feeds best in the warmer months but continues with reduced feeding in winter.
- Usually feeds on the bottom but in warmer weather can be caught at all depths and often prefers to eat at or near the water's surface. Can be seen cruising the surface as if sunbathing!
- An active fish that roams an entire fishery. They can be caught within a few centimetres of the bank or right out in the middle of the lake.
- Can feed 24 hours of the day. At some venues night fishing is the most effective way to catch them.
- Uses an extending telescopic mouth to suck in, forage and dig for food.
- Carp can often be seen jumping out of the water or rolling on the surface – commonly known as 'crashing' due to the size of the fish. This can be a key indicator of where they're feeding.
- Fish that are digging hard on the bottom, looking for food, often disturb lots of silt and mud. This colours the water and sends patches of bubbles fizzing to the surface – find these signs and you've found some carp to fish for.
- Strong, hard-fighting and long-lived – fish have been recorded over 40 years old, and some giants have grown to over 90lb!
- Carp come in several different variations. Common carp are fully covered in rows of small, similarly sized scales; 'mirror carp' are coated in random scatterings of variously sized scales; 'linear mirrors' have a row of scales running down the centre of each flank; 'fully scaled mirrors' are totally covered in randomly sized scales; and 'leather carp' are totally devoid of scales and have a smooth outer skin.

Below: A line of scales runs down the centre lateral line of a linear mirror.

Above: Fully scaled mirrors are covered in randomly sized scales.

Below: Leather carp are totally devoid of scales.

Barbel

This is one of the most powerful freshwater fish. It's naturally at home in rivers but has been successfully transferred to a growing number of lakes in recent years.

A lean, muscle-packed fish that fights hard and grows big, the barbel is highly sought-after amongst anglers – in fact many fishermen aspire to catch a barbel after learning how to catch smaller and less feisty fish first.

In rivers a pellet-stuffed swimfeeder is often the best way to catch barbel (Chapter 3 reveals all). However, it's possible to use a heavy float set-up to catch them too, and we provide details of that tactic in Chapter 2.

Above: The barbel is a sleek, strong river fish.

General characteristics

- The barbel's sloping head and streamlined body is the perfect shape for living in rivers. No matter how big a flood or how fast the water gets a barbel can still prosper.
- Generally prefers shallower, faster water rather than deep, slow sections of river.
- Often lives in or near weed beds, under riverside trees and bushes or in fast-water gravel runs.
- Uses probing barbules on the front of the mouth to locate food trapped in weed beds and between stones on the riverbed.
- Spade-shaped snout roots out tasty morsels by pushing aside rocks and weed to reveal the trapped meal.
- Underslung mouth is designed for feeding on or very near the riverbed.

Above: The underslung mouth is made for digging on the riverbed.

Dace

One of the smallest silverfish species, this fabulous fish is a wiry and tenacious fighter that often gives lightning-fast bites in the rivers and streams it calls home. A half-pounder is a big dace and a 1lb specimen is the fish of a lifetime.

These dainty feeders love maggots and casters, and although they can be caught using swimfeeder tactics a float is usually the way to succeed. You'll learn the best tactics to catch them in Chapter 2.

General characteristics

- Lives almost exclusively in rivers and streams. Prefers quicker water rather than deep slow sections of river.
- A small species that feeds at all depths, from surface down to riverbed.
- Because of their size they naturally feed on small food items, so anglers' baits must follow this lead.
- Feeds all year round but winter is often the best time to catch them, when they group into large shoals. As long as you can find them they'll feed in the coldest conditions.

Above: Dace are small, wiry river fish.

Pike

The top of the food chain, and the king predator in both still waters and rivers. Rows of razor-sharp teeth line its mouth – awesome weaponry that means curtains for the roach, bream and silverfish species that constitute its staple diet.

We look at specialist methods to catch pike in Chapter 6.

General characteristics

- Equally at home in rivers or lakes, but in moving water they're usually found in slower sections or in slacker areas on the edge of the main flow.
- To help locate prey they have a complex system of vibration sensors lining their head and jaw. This picks up the movement of fish, especially if they're sick or injured – the ruthless pike often picks on prey that's already in distress.

Above: With its mouth lined with rows of sharp teeth, the pike is an efficient predator.

- Binocular vision allows them to see their targets clearly, even in poor light conditions. Will feed 24 hours of the day but usually feeds best in daylight.
- Ambush-hunters, they lie in wait alongside cover such as a weed bed or sunken tree branch. Their mottled body colours guarantee excellent camouflage.
- When prey is spotted rapid acceleration is generated from the slender muscle-lined tail – speed of attack is a key weapon, and when a pike strikes at its prey a large swirl is often seen in the water.
- Will also scavenge for food and will eat dead fish that have sunk to the bottom. This is why deadbaits can be good for angling.
- Belying its fearsome appearance pike are quite delicate creatures that require careful handling. See Chapter 6.

Bream

This large slab-sided fish can be seen as the cattle of the freshwater world. They pack together in large shoals and feed by grazing the bottom of lakes, canals and rivers. They'll eat just about any bait you throw at them – maggots, casters, worms, pellets, meat, corn and boilies are all on the menu for a hungry pack of browsing bream.

While they can be caught using the float and pole tactics explained in Chapters 2 and 4 the best way to catch them is usually with a swimfeeder, so turn to Chapter 3 to find out how to fill your net with bream.

General characteristics

- Mostly found in lakes but also flourish in the deeper, slower sections of many rivers.
- Shoal fish that pack together in larger groupings and move en masse. They often have distinct patrol routes that are followed time and again – a successful angler needs to locate these paths.
- Their downward-sloping head and telescopic mouth are designed for feeding on the bottom, which is where they're most often caught.
- Feeds best in the warmer months but will continue with reduced feeding activity in the winter.
- Will feed 24 hours of the day. In lakes they prefer to feed when a wind is ruffling the surface, in rivers they prefer the water to have extra colour in it from recent rainfall. In hot, bright conditions they become evening, early morning or even nocturnal feeders.
- Not usually found near the bank, preferring to live in

Above: The underslung telescopic mouth is built for bottom-feeding.

deeper water further from the margins. Often seen 'rolling' on the surface.
- Not a fan of weed. They're most often found feeding in open areas of water where they can dig for food in gravel, soft mud or silt. Feeding fish often disturb tiny pockets of gas, which send bubbles to the surface – a key indicator to look for.

Below: Slab-sided bream are comfortable in slow-moving rivers and still waters.

Perch

One of the most striking of freshwater fish, perch sport vivid black and green striping and a sail-like dorsal fin adorned with sharp spines to protect them from larger predators.

Although not as obviously predatory as a pike because they don't have rows of teeth lining their lips, perch have a gaping mouth that's designed to take in small fish before they're passed back to throat teeth for crushing and swallowing. Perch don't just eat fish though, and worms, casters or maggots are all great baits to catch them with, whether you're using float, swimfeeder or pole techniques.

General characteristics

- Found in every type of fresh water, from the biggest reservoir to the smallest pond and most powerful river.
- Armed with a huge mouth that generates a

Above: Bold stripes, a spiky dorsal fin and a huge mouth distinguish the predatory perch.

powerful suction effect to draw small fish into its throat.

- Wonderful eyesight makes them active hunters, especially in low light conditions when they can see their prey but the prey can't see them.
- Camouflage striping helps them blend into background cover such as trees, bushes or boat moorings. They can then ambush passing fish.
- Tremendously active hunters that often feed in packs to chase down and corral shoals of small fish. Look for explosions of tiny fish on the surface of the water – the chances are they're being chased by hungry perch!
- Feeds well all year round.
- A lover of natural food items rather than man-made baits. Maggots, casters and worms are liked by perch just as much as the small fish they naturally feed on.

Tench

A unique coarse fish with silky smooth skin that's usually found in still waters or slow-moving rivers and feeds best during the warmer months.

Tench are a species that feeds primarily on the lake bed and has a wide-ranging appetite that includes just about all the main fishing baits. Though they often feed in the margins of a lake they also roam open water and so can be caught using float, pole and swimfeeder tactics alike.

General characteristics

- A warm-weather species that almost hibernates in winter.
- Mainly a lake and canal fish but can also survive in deep, slow-moving rivers and drains.
- Often feeds best close to the bank where there's plenty of cover. Beds of rushes, lily pads, weed beds and the shade of overhanging trees are all favoured haunts.
- Mostly a fish that feeds on the lake bed. They use their mouths to dig for food, a process that sends a shower of

Right: Male tench have larger spoon-shaped pectoral fins and a distinctive pectoral muscle, females have small pectoral fins.

Above: Smooth-skinned and powerful fighters, tench are fabulous fish.

tiny pin-prick bubbles on a journey to the surface, where they appear as a telltale patch. This is often called 'fizzing'.
- In traditional lakes they feed best in low light conditions at dawn or in the evening. In large man-made gravel pits tench feed well in broad daylight.
- A strong, hard-fighting fish, it uses its broad tail and fins to fight every inch of the way to the net. A true anglers' favourite!

Crucian carp

A very different type of fish to the carp already described, the crucian is a much smaller disc-shaped species that behaves in a totally different way to its distant relatives.

With their flanks painted deep gold, and striking orange fins adding another splash of rich colour, the muscular crucian is one of the most attractive coarse fish and also one of the most challenging to catch due to its fussy feeding style. Sensitive waggler float tactics (see Chapter 2) can be good, but probably the best way to catch crucian carp is with a delicate pole set-up, outlined in Chapter 4.

General characteristics

- Found almost entirely in still waters, crucians almost hibernate once the end of autumn arrives.
- They feed almost exclusively on the lake bed, picking daintily at small food items and turning over the silt as they try to unearth bloodworms and other tiny bugs. This means crucians often send up a few tiny bubbles to the surface, an easily missed but key piece of evidence to locate feeding areas.
- Crucians are also one of the most delicate feeders. In comparison to carp, tench and bream that suck up

Above: Golden and glistening, crucians are delicate feeders and one of the most beautiful coarse fish.

morsels of food in a mouth designed like a hoover, crucians feed in a much more measured way. They pick up each piece of food in their lips, and they tend to be far more cautious and sensitive to fishing tackle. As a general rule anyone who can consistently catch crucian carp deserves a pat on the back!

Gudgeon

Looking like a miniature barbel, the gudgeon is a small streamlined species that can be found in just about every river and canal, as well as farm ponds and natural lakes everywhere.

The growth of man-made commercial fisheries has done little to promote this species, and few hold many gudgeon, so if you want to catch one you must head for natural venues. Maggots are the number one gudgeon bait.

General characteristics

- One of the smallest species, and was once the first fish that many anglers caught.
- An underslung mouth means they're designed for feeding on the bottom of lakes, canals and rivers.
- Will feed throughout the year but in recent years has suffered a decline in numbers due to over-predation and greater man-management of fisheries.

Below: These small fish are often found in ponds and canals.

Chub

Like barbel, chub are primarily a river species that has latterly spread to still waters. A greedy fish that eats a huge range of angling baits, chub are also powerful and fight hard, especially when hooked in the fast water conditions they find especially attractive.

Special float tactics are the best way to catch these fish. In Chapter 2 we reveal the rigs and baits that work best to tempt them, while in Chapter 3 we provide ideas that can be brilliant for tricking chub.

Above: Bold and brassy, the chub is a cautious but greedy fish that prospers in rivers and lakes.

General characteristics

- Mostly found in rivers, especially the faster and shallower sections rather than the deep, slow parts. They feed right through the year and will often feed in very cold conditions when other fish have stopped.
- They usually live between beds of streamer weed, under overhanging trees and bushes or beneath tangles of roots and rafts of collected debris. Can also be found pointing head upstream on gravel runs.
- They're mainly sight feeders that dart out from under cover to snatch items of food whizzing downstream on the current. This means they prefer to feed in relatively clear water conditions, although a smellier bait can produce good results when a river is coloured with rainwater as chub also have a good sense of smell.
- They have a huge gaping mouth and an appetite to match. Large throat teeth help devour small fish, slugs, worms or just about any bait the angler can think of.
- Although greed can make them voracious feeders they're also very wary, especially in small rivers and streams where they're easily alerted by clumsy movement and excessive noise. Once spooked they seek cover or leave the area.

Rudd

Bright red fins and a metallic green hue to their vibrant golden scales make rudd one of the most beautiful and popular coarse fish.

Although they can be caught on the lake bed with a swimfeeder, a more successful method is usually a pole or float tactic that allows the bait to sink slowly.

General characteristics

- Though the upward-sloping mouth indicates that rudd prefer to feed off the bottom, in fact they often feed at or near to the surface, especially in summer when flies hatch and surface bugs provide an abundance of their natural food.
- A delicate feeder with a small mouth, they eat small items of food, so you've got to keep your baits small.
- Mainly a warm-weather fish, they can nevertheless be caught in winter, especially during milder spells when they briefly become more active.
- Almost exclusively found in stillwater lakes and ponds, they often feed best in bright, warm conditions. Look for shoals of rudd dimpling the surface of the water as they snatch bugs and grubs trapped in the surface film.

Left: Vividly coloured scales and fins characterise the stunning rudd, which often feeds in the middle to upper layers.

Roach

One of the most common species in every type of fresh water, the silver-flanked roach is often mistaken for rudd or small bream, though the red fins, more beak-shaped mouth and different-shaped dorsal and anal fins should help you to identify them.

Roach are often one of the first fish anglers catch, probably because they're so numerous and so widespread, and also because they love commonly used baits such as maggots, casters, worms and small pieces of bread. The tactics explained in Chapters 2 to 4 will show you how to catch them.

General characteristics

- Found in almost every lake, canal and river. In moving water they prefer slow to medium-paced water rather than fast or turbulent water.
- A fish that feeds all year round. They often become easier to catch in colder months when other silverfish species and small fish are much less active, so the small baits roach prefer can be used without the risk of interception by others.
- Roach feed at all depths although as a general rule they tend to feed in the upper layers during the warmer months. In winter they drift closer to the bottom, where they do the bulk of their feeding.
- A shoal fish that gathers into large groups, they can be

Above: One of the most popular coarse fish, roach sport silver scales tinged with a deep metallic blue.

caught close to the bank. However, as a key prey of pike and other predators they're very cautious and will often gather in deeper water away from the margins and any riverside disturbance.
- They can also be erratic feeders in bright conditions, especially when the water is very clear, as they're much more exposed to predation by pike, perch and birds like cormorants, grebes and herons. In these conditions they feed best early in the morning or late in the evening. In rivers they tend to feed best after rainfall has given the flow a tinge of extra colour as soil is washed off the land.

Eel

One of the most enigmatic and elusive freshwater fish, the life of the eel is one of the last underwater mysteries left to be thoroughly investigated.

While the small, writhing eels caught in just about every river, stream, canal and natural lake can give anglers nightmares when it comes to unhooking them, the bigger predatory specimens represent one of angling's toughest challenges.

Notoriously fussy eaters, tremendously hard-fighting and very difficult to locate, a specimen eel is one of the greatest of all coarse fish.

General characteristics

- Few hard facts are known about the breeding cycle of the eel although it is suspected they migrate between salt water and fresh water to breed in the Sargasso Sea. However, some scientists believe this is a fanciful notion!
- The thin-headed 'bootlace' eels eat just about any small item of food and can be caught on basic fishing baits such as worms and maggots.

- As they get older many eels become increasingly predatory and their head shape alters as they develop larger jaws and a wider, flatter head. Such predators also become increasingly nocturnal in their feeding habits.

Above: Eels are a mystery fish that turn predatory as they get bigger.

Catfish

One of the most distinctive fish and one that's growing in popularity amongst anglers due to the sheer size it can attain and the power of the fight it can unleash. Found throughout the rivers of Europe, 'cats' have also been introduced to many lakes, where they've prospered.

In the wild they're a fish-eating predator, but in many managed fisheries they've developed a taste for the man-made baits used by carp anglers and can now be caught using many of the tactics featured in Chapter 5.

General characteristics

- The tiny eyes are a clue to the fact that the catfish is almost blind.
- They rely on a keen sense of smell and the long and sensitive whiskers at the front of their heads to locate dead fish or bait they can scavenge on.
- Catfish also have a super-sensitive motion sensor that can pinpoint the vibrations of prey fish, especially those that are injured or in distress. Pads of rough sandpaper-like teeth help them grab and grip prey fish before they're crushed and swallowed. They're one of the few fish to have a stomach, so they tend to feed in binges before lying up to digest their food.
- Catfish feed almost exclusively during the warmer months, with the peak of summer being the key feeding season. They all but hibernate in the winter and completely shut down feeding activity. Don't waste time catfishing in the cold!
- Most catfish captures occur in low light conditions, either at night, in the evening, or during the early hours of the morning.

Above: Catfish are hugely powerful predators that fight hard and grow big.

Above: Pads of rough teeth line their mouth and throat to help catfish grab their prey.

Below: Catfish use these long whiskers to sense the movement of prey fish and pick up the smell of food.

Zander

Originally referred to as the 'pikeperch' due to its combination of the characteristics found in those predatory species, the zander is a distinct and fearsome killing machine in its own right.

Becoming more widespread as it populates more river systems and is stocked in lakes, the zander is fished for in a very similar fashion to pike and the tactics described in Chapter 6 will give you a good grounding to catch them.

General characteristics

- Owners of the best eyes amongst freshwater species, they use their awesome vision to attack prey at night and in low light conditions when they can't be spotted by their victims.
- A keen sense of smell also helps them locate dead fish.
- They're usually caught at night, when they do the vast majority of their feeding.
- Zander don't have the many rows of small gripping teeth that pike possess. Instead they have a few lethal fangs at the front and side of their jaws that are designed to puncture and slice through fish flesh, causing it massive injury. Even if its targeted prey momentarily escapes the grip of a zander it's likely to be so badly injured that it won't get very far.

Right: Razor-sharp daggers for teeth and keen eyesight give the zander an edge when hunting.

Above: A deadly predator, zander feed on small silverfish like roach and bream.

Grayling

A wiry and hard-fighting fish that's mainly found in fast-flowing rivers. Often fished for by game anglers with fly fishing tackle, the grayling can also be caught with coarse fishing kit. They're particularly sought after by float anglers, who trot with stick floats to tempt them.

General characteristics

- A large sail-like dorsal fin running along the top of the grayling's back is the most obvious feature of this unusual fish.
- Tiny multicoloured scales cover the fish, and depending on how the light catches them the fish can appear very silver or shot with rich purple colouration.
- Grayling are a very muscular fish that fight very hard for their size. They also sport a small, beak-shaped mouth.

Below: Grayling sport spectacular colouration and a huge dorsal fin.

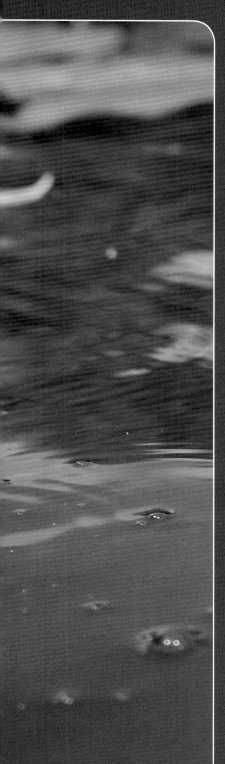

FLOAT FISHING

Essential kit for stillwater float fishing	24
Waggler fishing kit essential extras	32
The four golden rules of waggler fishing	34
Setting up a waggler rig	36
Plumbing the depth	38
Three essential waggler rigs	40
Casting a float	41
Feeding on the float	42
Striking and landing fish	44
Waggler float fishing tips	46
The pellet waggler	48
Learning the stick float	51
Combating fast water	53
Easily hooked	54
Baiting your hook	56

There are lots of different floats that are all designed to do different jobs.

Float fishing with a rod, reel and line is what most people imagine coarse angling to be, and it's probably the method that most newcomers to the sport begin with.

In this chapter we'll look at the tackle you need, how you put it together, and how you use it in a host of different scenarios, because one of the great strengths of float fishing is that it's very adaptable to any type of venue.

Whether you're fishing in a tiny pond, a huge lake or a roaring river, there's a float to suit every situation in which you might find yourself, and in this section we'll study how to vary the way you use a float in order to catch fish regardless of the water conditions.

Float fishing is an art form and even the most experienced anglers can learn new skills. However, it needn't be a technique to be scared of – once you've learned a few basics you'll soon be regularly catching fish on the float.

What's more, once you've learned how to float fish the core skills you gain will stand you in good stead for any other type of coarse fishing you move on to. That's why it's the first technical chapter in this manual. Once you've learned how to catch fish on the float the rest will come easily.

To kick off this chapter we'll start by looking at the tackle you need to float fish in still water, as it's far easier to learn in a lake, reservoir or pond than a raging river. At the end of the section we'll investigate the changes you need to make to your approach if you're trying to catch fish in moving water.

Essential kit for stillwater float fishing

Picking the right rod

There are so many float rods on the market that choosing one can be very confusing. Different lengths are available, they can be made out of different materials, and they can bend in a

different manner (called the 'action' of the rod) when they're put under a loading for casting or playing a fish.

To simplify the choice it's essential to spend time talking to your local tackle shop dealer. They're usually very experienced anglers themselves and will provide you with good advice and talk you through the minefield of rod choices.

While Internet shopping might seem like a good idea because of the savings you can make, getting to know a reliable local dealer will prove to be a massive help to anyone learning to fish. Not only do they provide a more personal service and remove confusion by answering any questions you may have, but they're also a great source of information about the fisheries you're likely to visit.

Also, it stands to reason that if you become a valued customer a dealer will be more willing to offer you extra help on the best places to fish, the baits you'll need and any extra gems of information that might help you catch a few more fish at a particular venue.

To give you a starting point for your discussions, a rod 12ft to 13ft long is usually what you want, and it should be made from carbon rather than glass fibre or a composite of the two materials. This means the rod will be lightweight and sensitive so that you can use it all day without your arms aching.

Left: To get a rod that suits your needs, head for a tackle shop and talk to the dealer.

Above and right: Screw-down reel seats allow you to fix the reel firmly to the handle.

Look for a rod with a screw-down reel seat on the handle that firmly anchors the reel, and ensure that the guides running down the rod have a ceramic inner ring so that the line passes through them smoothly. This aids casting performance and the playing of large fish.

Finally, look at the action of the rod itself and advise the dealer as best you can of the fisheries you intend to visit. If the waters you're fishing hold lots of smaller fish species and few bigger carp and tench, then a softer action rod that bends smoothly under a light loading will be the best choice. These lightweight and responsive rods are often labelled as 'Match' rods due to their historical use in competition angling for small fish.

However, if the lake you're fishing is home to lots of larger and hard-fighting fish such as carp and tench you need to use a more powerful rod with a beefier action. These are often labelled 'Power' or 'Carp' float rods. In many modern managed fisheries where the dominant species are 3lb to 10lb carp, this powerful style of float rod is a more suitable choice, and they've become very popular. It's significant that most new rods launched in recent years have been power models with an action designed to cope with bigger fish.

As I said in the introduction to this manual, fishing has undergone huge changes in recent years, and the reality of fishing on managed fisheries is that large carp and tench will soon be picking up your bait and giving you a battle royal. So whereas it might have taken previous generations of anglers many years to catch a large carp the great news is that you'll soon be doing it on a regular basis, so you need to buy the right tackle for the job!

Above: You need to select rods that suit the size of the fish you're likely to catch.

Below: A power float rod can be used to land large fish on the float.

Above: A small, solid reel made with a graphite or alloy metal body and good gearing should last for years.

Teaming up the rod with the right reel

The reel to go with your float rod should be what's called a 'fixed spool' type. This means that as you turn the reel handle to retrieve line and wrap it on to the reel the spool doesn't revolve but just moves up and down to ensure the line is laid smoothly on to it.

Just as the price of rods has fallen in recent years so the cost of reels has tumbled, and it's now possible to buy a good-quality reel at a very affordable price. Always remember, though, that what a reel looks like on the outside is relatively unimportant – it's the gearing inside that does all the work, and some reels are made of sterner stuff than others.

What you're looking for is a reel that will last, so for starters you should go for one that has a graphite or alloy metal body rather than being a plastic construction. These are much tougher and withstand bangs and bumps better. They also give the reel a more rigid, solid feel.

Also ask the tackle dealer about the quality of the internal bearings and gearing. Just buying a reel with the largest number of bearings, for example, doesn't necessarily

guarantee that you get the best product. If the bearings are poor quality it doesn't matter how many there are in the reel.

The quality of the internal guts of a reel is also likely to be reflected in the quality of the 'drag' (also called a 'clutch') that will be fitted to it. Think of the drag as a tensioning device that will resist the pull of a hooked fish tugging on the line – the slacker it is the easier it will be for the fish to 'run' away from you.

By altering the tension placed on the drag you can control how a large fish pulls line off the reel. As we'll see later this plays a vital role in successfully landing larger specimens and stops them breaking your line when they rush off. The drag on a reel should always be set slack enough to release line before its breaking point is reached, to reduce fish and tackle losses.

Also check out the handle on a reel. There are many different shapes and materials you can go for, and it's essential that the handle fits comfortably in your hand. Such choices are entirely individual, which is another good reason for buying a reel from a local shop where you can actually try it out first.

Finally, it's also worth buying a reel that's supplied with two interchangeable spools as this allows you to load different breaking strains of line on to them so that you can use the same reel for different tasks, such as float fishing and swimfeeder fishing.

Ideally the reel you buy should have spools of differing depths so that they take different capacities of line – a deep spool is best for swimfeeder fishing (see Chapter 3) while a shallow spool (often called a 'match' spool) is better for float fishing, as you generally fish at much shorter range and require less line to be wound on to it.

In my experience it's better to buy a product made by a reputable company like Shimano, Daiwa or Abu, as they have decades of experience in making reels and their internal workings are strong and reliable. These firms all make top-quality reels, and as a rule you get what you pay for. As with most things in life, buying the cheapest product is likely to work out more expensive in the long run, and while you don't need to break the bank to buy the very best kit, it's almost always worth buying a middle-of-the-range reel that has been built to last.

Remember that your reel is the workhorse of your float tackle, with a major role in cranking in the fish you hook. If it isn't up to the task the gearing will fail and you'll soon be buying a replacement.

Above: The drag or clutch on a reel is set by a dial on the front of the spool or at the rear of the reel.

Below: Make sure that the handle is comfortable to hold.

Above: There are lots of different lines to choose from. Ask your tackle dealer which type you should pick.

Filling the reel with line

Walk into any tackle shop and you're likely to be met with a bewildering choice of different brands of nylon line in a wide range of different breaking strains – which one do you choose?

It's pointless recommending a specific brand in this book because products change almost constantly. What you need to do is tell the tackle dealer that you're looking for a dependable reel line for float fishing. They should then be able to offer you a range of lines at different prices for you to choose from.

Ideally you're looking for a limp, soft line that doesn't leap off its drum in wiry coils. Presuming that you're going to be doing most of your fishing on lakes it's also vital that it sinks. Some lines actually float like corks, and these are bad news for stillwater fishing – the wind will grab a line laying on the surface and drag your float all over the lake! Not only will this pull your rig away from the spot that you should be

Below: Floating lines are good for trotting a float in rivers but not for stillwater waggler float fishing.

feeding with extra bait, it will also make your hookbait behave suspiciously – a fish isn't going to chase after the one bait that's running away when all the other food items are stationary. They might be fish but they're not totally stupid!

The next thing you need to decide on is the breaking strain of the line. Every line will be labelled with its diameter and strength (or breaking strain), and as you'd imagine, the thicker the line is the stronger it becomes. However, one of the most common mistakes that learning anglers repeatedly make is to choose line that's far stronger than they require.

In fact it's very important that you don't automatically pick a line with a breaking strain of 8lb to 10lb. While it might seem logical to choose a tow rope the fish can't easily break you'll find it's also very thick and wiry, and this will massively hinder your ability to cast and control a lightweight float. A heavy duty line will also affect the way your float and bait behaves in the water, and fish will soon be able to spot that bait is attached to a rig made of hefty material.

The simple fact is that many newcomers to float fishing don't catch many fish simply because they choose reel line (also called mainline) which is far too thick and strong. In all but the most extreme circumstances (*ie* when you're fishing for really big fish) a reel line of 3lb to 5lb will do the job – if the water you're going to fish contains roach, bream, perch, small tench and little carp a 3lb breaking-strain line will suffice, but if you're likely to encounter larger fish you should step up to a 4lb or 5lb line.

While you might end up catching fish heavier than the stated breaking strain of the line the cushioning effect of the rod bending usually stops a specimen exerting its full weight on it. This means that it's perfectly possible to land a 10lb fish on line that breaks at 4lb.

The picture sequence opposite is a step-by-step guide to loading line on your reel. Follow this and you're almost ready to go fishing; all you need to do is get some floats and a few bits of tackle to go with it.

Below: You need to pick the right breaking strain of line when float fishing – this product is ideal for waggler fishing.

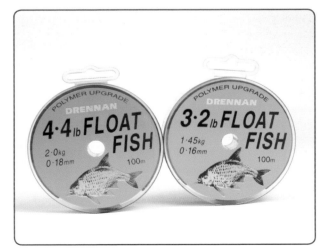

1 Soak your spool of mainline in warm water for an hour – it'll make it less springy. Then attach the mainline to the spool using the sliding uni-knot shown. Before tightening the knot push it to the base of the spool and snip off the tag end, leaving at least an inch of line.

2 Get someone to hold the spool and pinch the line with a piece of cloth or packing foam. Don't hold it in a vice-like grip – it should be held with a steady pressure. Wind ten metres of line on to the reel.

3 Now comes the crucial bit. You should aim to wind the line on to the reel in the same direction as it was put on to the spool holding it to stop it twisting. Open the bail arm on the reel, pull off an arm's length of line and give it a tug.

4 Let the line drop, and if it's been wound on the reel in the right direction it should be limp and untwisted and will droop in a smooth U shape like this.

5 However, if the line spins and twists around itself like this you need to change the direction in which it's being wound on to the reel.

It's essential that you fill the spool correctly. If you underfill it so that there's a large lip above the line you'll find it difficult to cast very far as the line will drag over the edge of the spool. On the other hand, if you overfill the reel so that line is bulging on the spool you'll suffer from explosions of nylon as the coils tumble over each other and cause the nightmare of a bird's nest of tangled line at the reel.

What you're actually looking to do is fill the spool to just below its front edge. Line should then peel off it smoothly to maximise your casting performance.

Below: It's worth taking time to load your reel with untwisted line. Fill it to just below the lip of the spool to maximise casting performance.

6 Do this by turning round the spool of line so that its rear is facing the reel. Wind ten metres more of line on to the reel and repeat the test outlined previously.

7 If the line still twists turn the spool side-on to the reel and turn the handle. Test the twist again to see which position is the best way to hold the spool. Twisted line is far more likely to cause tangles.

Stillwater floats explained

There are dozens of different float patterns available for fishing in still waters, but the three main types are explained here.

To start with you don't need to buy too many – a few straight and insert wagglers will do. A collection of floats is something most anglers build slowly over many years as they fish different venues that require slightly different patterns and sizes of float.

Below: There are lots of different patterns and sizes of waggler floats but the main ones are straights and inserts.

The straight waggler

This is the most basic still-water float and one you must have in your tackle box. It's attached to the line through the bottom of the float so that it waggles on the nylon – hence its name.

It's usually made from a single length of peacock quill, reed stem or clear plastic tubing, and like all floats it has its shotting capacity stamped on the side. This is an estimation of the amount of split shot weights you'll need to pinch on to the line to counter the buoyancy of the float and make it sit correctly in the water so that only the coloured tip is visible.

How this works will soon be described, but for now all you need to know is that the bigger the float is and the more shot it will support the further it can be cast into the water.

A common mistake that learning anglers make is to choose floats that are far too big, too buoyant and take too much split shot – they hit the water like a brick and any fish that aren't scared away will struggle to pull the float under to register a bite. Float fishing when done correctly is a technique based on finesse and delicacy, not brute force!

A few floats with a 2AAA to 4AAA shotting capacity will suffice to get you started.

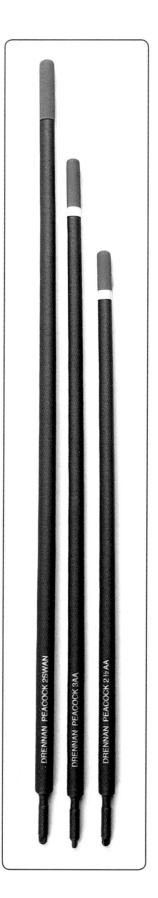

Right: Straight waggler floats are made with a single length of peacock quill or plastic tubing.

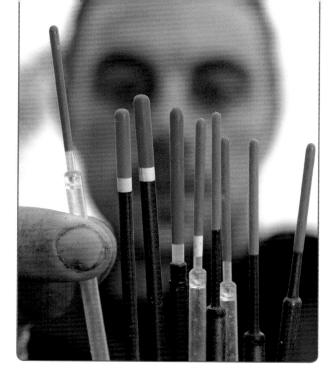

Above: The thin tip of an insert float is more sensitive than a straight waggler.

Above: All types of waggler floats should be marked with the capacity of shot that needs to be attached to the line to make the float sit properly in the water.

The insert waggler

This is a slight variation on the standard straight waggler. Instead of the float being made from a single piece of quill or plastic the insert is a two-piece construction in which a slender tip is plugged (or inserted) into a thicker body. The reason for doing this is that the thinner tip is more easily pulled under the water by a fish picking up the bait on your hook. This makes the float more sensitive, as it registers bites more quickly and will even show interest from shy-biting species like roach and crucian carp that might not pull the thick-tipped straight waggler under the surface.

Many modern insert floats also allow you to change the tip in a few seconds, which can help combat changing light conditions or reflections that might make a particular colour of tip hard to see.

As a general rule orange and yellow-tipped floats are easier to see in shaded 'dark' water, whereas a black- or red-tipped float shows up well in full sunlight, when the water has a 'white' reflection.

The loaded waggler

This is simply a waggler float with a large part of its shotting capacity built into its base in order to reduce the amount of shot you need to pinch on to the line. While they're not essential, loaded floats do have two advantages.

First, they tend to cast well because the loading is built aerodynamically into the float.

And second, each time you pinch a split shot on to the reel line you potentially weaken it a small amount – consequently the fewer shot you have to attach to the line, the more of the line's breaking strain you'll preserve.

Below: Their specially weighted base gives loaded wagglers an aerodynamic profile for better casting.

Waggler fishing kit essential extras

Above: You need to get different sizes of split shot to use with waggler floats.

If picking the correct rod, reel, line and floats provides the right foundation for successful coarse fishing, then the extra bits of kit shown here provide the bricks you'll need in order to build on that.

1 Split shot

You'll need a range of split shot to attach to the line your float will sit on. Ideally you should buy a multi-dispenser that contains large SSG and AAA shot right down to small No.8 shot. Tubs can be bought containing individual sizes of shot so that you can refill your dispenser, and if your eyesight and manual dexterity are up to the job of putting really small shot on the line it's also worth buying a tub of No 10 shot. These tiny 'dust shot' are great for fine-tuning float and pole rigs.

The comparison chart (above right) provides a rundown of shot sizes and weights. You'll notice how the size and weight of shot diminishes as the number applied to it gets higher – a No.1 shot is bigger and heavier than a No.10 shot.

Left: Non-toxic shot are essential, and you need to understand how much the different sizes weigh.

Below: These tubs hold the main sizes of shot that you'll need. The table shows how the different sizes compare to each other.

Your guide to split shot weights

SSG = 2 x AAA shot (1.6g)
AAA = 2 x BB shot (0.8g)
BB = 2 x No.4 shot (0.4g)
No.1 = 3 x No.6 shot (0.3g)
No.3 = 2 x No.6 shot (0.25g)
No.4 = 3 x No.9 shot (0.2g)
No.5 = 2 x No.8 shot (0.15g)
No.6 = 2 x No.10 shot (0.1g)
No.8 = 0.06g
No.10 = 0.04g

Above: Ready-tied hooks-to-nylon are cheap and offer a secure link between your reel line and a hooked fish.

2 Hooks-to-nylon

At the bottom of a float rig will be a short length of line carrying the hook. This is called the hooklength, hooklink, trace, tail or hook-to-nylon. All five descriptions mean exactly the same thing!

As a general rule this short length is slightly lighter in breaking strain than the reel line so that if the rig becomes trapped in an underwater obstruction, or a fish manages to break the line, only the end tackle is lost, and not the entire rig complete with float and metres of nylon.

While you can tie these short links yourself it's easier if you buy them ready-tied from a reputable firm such as Drennan, Middy, Maver or Preston Innovations. Sold in small card envelopes containing individual hooklinks that are slipped inside a plastic sleeve, well tied hooks-to-nylon make float fishing easy, so it's worth stocking up on a few packets.

Buy barbless hooks in sizes 14 to 20 with breaking strains of 5lb to 2.5lb.

3 Float adaptors

These brilliant silicone rubber sleeves make it easier to attach the float to the reel line and far quicker to switch floats during your fishing session – for instance when the wind picks up and you have to use a bigger float to reach the area you've been

fishing. An adaptor means that changing floats becomes a matter of simply unplugging one float and plugging in another, rather than having to retackle the entire rig. They cost just a few pence and are essential, as you'll see in the next few pages.

4 Plummet

This small weight is one of the most underused pieces of tackle there is, but if you're going to become a successful float fisher it's essential that you use one every time you prepare to cast a float.

On pages 38/39 you'll see how to use this anonymous-looking lump of metal to measure (or plumb) the depth of the water in front of you. It's vital that every time you go fishing you know exactly how deep the area you're fishing is, so that you can place your bait precisely on the bottom or at any other depth you want to fish to.

There are lots of different plummets available. Rather than one of the clip-on varieties, which can damage fine line, I'd recommend that you use one with an eye at the top and a foam or cork base for the hook to sink into.

Plummets are really cheap but are worth their weight in gold to any float angler.

Below: These cheap gadgets are essential if you want to simplify attaching and changing floats during a fishing session.

Below: A plummet is essential for plumbing the depth of water you're float fishing into – never fish without using one!

The four golden rules of waggler fishing

Now that you've got the right tackle you're nearly ready to set up a waggler float rig and get fishing. However, before you gallop on and repeat the mistakes thousands of other learning anglers have made, and still make, it's essential that you memorise four simple rules regarding how you set up a waggler float.

Where and how you put your split shot on the line is something lots of anglers get confused about – even people who've been fishing for many years get it wrong. But how the shot are used makes a big difference to how your float performs and how many fish you'll catch with it.

These four rules will help you get it right. They aren't complicated, or difficult to follow – in fact it's as easy to stick to them and do the job correctly as it is to do it incorrectly, so you might as well do it right from the outset!

1 The 75% rule

This is the minimum percentage of the shotting capacity that should be placed at the base of the float. A waggler float should always 'boss' the rest of the rig when you cast, and putting at least three-quarters of the split shot weights at the

bottom of the float adaptor ensures that this happens – the float will fly through the air first, dragging the rest of the line and hook behind it.

Bulking the shot near the float means that it will also cast in a straight line, be less affected by side-wind, and will maximise your casting distance.

Don't think that you can only put 75% of the shot at the float – this is a minimum, not a maximum, requirement and with many shotting patterns you'll place even more than this near the float.

2 Increase the gap

Every angler suffers from tangles at some time or other, and it will happen to you as you learn to fish, but as you become more proficient it will become far less of a problem. Don't let tangles bother you – even the best anglers suffer from them.

However, you can take steps to reduce tangles. Following the 75% rule is one of them, and another key way to cut the chances of tangling your rig on the cast is to increase the distance between the shot spread out in the bottom half of your rig.

These small shot are often called 'droppers', as they ensure the hookbait has a smooth fall (or drop) through the last part of its descent, and the distance between each shot should increase as you come up the line from the hook. For example, if the bottom shot is placed eight inches (20cm) above the hook, the next shot should be ten inches (25cm) above that, and a third shot should then be placed at least twelve inches (30cm) higher still.

This shotting pattern stops the rig tumbling through the air when you cast and lays it out in a straight line when it hits the water. This reduces the chance of the shot hitting each other or the float and becoming a tangled mess.

3 The No.8 rule

It's essential that you add enough weight to the line to dot the float tip right. This is one of the most common mistakes made by many experienced and inexperienced anglers alike.

If you leave a large amount of the float tip showing above the water, so that it looks more like a lighthouse than a pin-prick of float tip, it will be far harder for the fish to pull

Left: At least three-quarters of the shotting capacity marked on the side of the float should be placed at the base of the float next to the float adaptor.

it under the water when they pick up your bait. And if your float just dips a little, rather than disappearing altogether, you're far less likely to strike at the bite and you'll miss the fish.

Furthermore many shy-biting species, especially roach, crucian carp and tench, can feel the resistance offered by a large section of float tip poking above the water when they pick up your bait. This is often enough to make them spit out the bait in the blink of an eye – and you've just missed your chance to catch a fish.

However, if you add enough shot to the rig to dot the float right down so that just a tiny part shows above the surface it will be far less buoyant and the resistance it offers will be greatly reduced.

The No.8 rule is a great way to ensure that you've shotted the float correctly. Quite simply if you've dotted the float down so much that adding another small No.8 shot to the line will cause the float to sink under the water you've got the rig spot on. Only a tiny bit of the float will be visible and a fish will only have to mouth your bait to pull the float under and alert you to a bite – your rig has become a super-sensitive set-up that'll catch you lots of fish.

4 The fold test

This is a great tip and like several of the rules on this page it comes directly from master float angler and former world champion Tommy Pickering – he'd be one of the first names on my list if I had to have someone catch me a fish to save my life!

The picture below shows Tom's fold test for a waggler rig, a super simple rule that reduces tangles massively. He believes that all the small dropper shot strung out down the line below a float must be positioned in the bottom half of the rig. For example, if you were fishing in 6ft (1.8m) of water the first dropper shot should be 3ft 4in (1.0m) below the float. Having the weight of the droppers isolated in the lower section in this way strings out the rig on the cast and stops the line wrapping round the float.

To ensure that you've got your rig set up correctly there's an easy test you can do that takes just a couple of seconds. Simply tighten the line and pinch the first dropper shot below the float between your thumb and first finger, then keeping the line tight grab the hook in your other hand and fold it back towards the float.

The hook must not touch or go past the locking shot that fix the float to the line. If it does, push the first dropper shot towards the hook. Repeat the test until the hook comes up short of the float by a few inches.

THE FOUR GOLDEN RULES OF WAGGLER FISHING

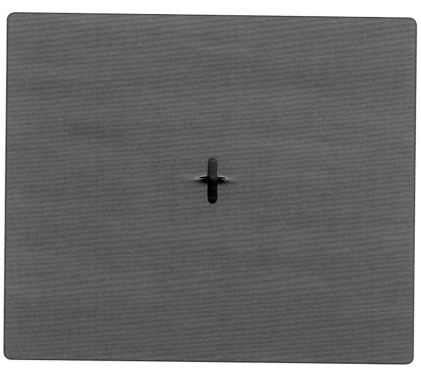

Above: Enough weight should be added to the line so that if you add one more No 8 shot the float will pull under. Dotting down the float like this makes it more sensitive.

Below: Pinch the first dropper shot and the hook and fold the line back towards the float – the hook should come up short of it.

Are you ready to go fishing yet?

Yes, I thought so! You've got your rod, reel, line, floats and four bits of vital kit, plus a few rules that will guide how you use them. Now you're ready to slot everything together and catch a fish on the float.

Over the next few pages we'll put the tackle jigsaw together, showing you how to set up a float rig, plumb the depth, cast the float, feed the swim and catch a fish. Don't worry, it's easy!

35

Setting up a waggler rig

This step-by-step guide shows you everything you need to know in order to combine the key items of your tackle to create a basic float fishing rig prior to plumbing the depth.

1 Remove the rod from its protective bag and gently push the sections together. Most 12ft or 13ft rods are supplied in three sections with two joints. These should be slotted together firmly, but don't jam them hard against each other – this can damage the carbon.

2 Ensure that the rod rings (otherwise known as guides) are in a straight line. If they're off-centre your casting performance will be hugely restricted.

3 Select your reel and secure it firmly to the rod via the screw-down seat. You don't want it dropping off the rod halfway through a battle with a big fish!

4 Open the bail arm on the reel and release the line from the clip on the side of the spool.

5 Pull line off the reel, thread it through the centre of each rod ring and pull it back down to the reel seat. Close the bail arm.

6 Moisten the end of the float and push it into the silicone float adaptor. Moistening the base helps it slide into the adaptor.

7 Run the line through the tiny hole in the end of the float adaptor. This vital gadget helps you change floats during a fishing session, as you can simply pull the float out and replace it with another one without having to tackle up again.

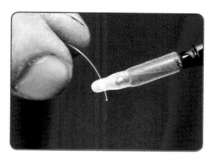

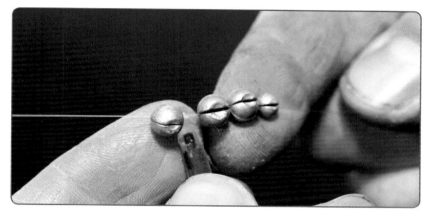

8 Slide the float a few feet up the line. Read the shotting capacity on the float and lock the float in place by pinching the appropriate split shot at its base, remembering the 75% rule as you do so – the quantity of the shotting capacity that should be placed at the base of the float.

9 At this point ensure that the float is well under-shotted by attaching less shot to the line than the shotting capacity stated on the side of the float. This is essential to help accurate plumbing of the depth with a plummet (see pages 38/39). Drop the float in the water and ensure that an inch or more of the tip is standing proud. This will help with the depth-plumbing process.

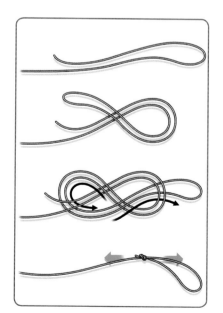

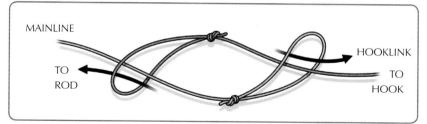

11 Attach the reel line to a hook-to-nylon following the loop-to-loop knot illustrated. Note how the hook passes through the loop on the reel line NOT the loop on the hooklink.

10 Tie a small figure-of-eight loop in the bottom of the mainline.

That's the first phase of the rig constructed. That wasn't too difficult, was it?

Now we're going to move on and show you how to plumb the depth of the water with the rig. Though many anglers ignore this vital skill it's essential that you don't make this mistake. It's a process that takes you only a few minutes at the start of every float fishing trip but it has a dramatic effect on what you catch.

The most successful anglers always plumb the depth before they start fishing.

Plumbing the depth

This step-by-step sequence will show you how to measure the depth of the water in front of the place (often called a 'peg' or 'swim') that you've decided to fish.

A key thing to take note of is that the procedure for casting a rig with a plummet attached to it differs slightly from how you cast a float rig with a baited hook. This is because of the extra weight attached to the hook.

Page 41 provides details of how you cast a float and sink the line when the plumbing has been completed.

Right: Before fishing, the best anglers always plumb the depth. This is 2008 World Champion William Raison attaching a plummet.

1 Thread your hook through the eye on the top of the plummet and ease the point into the cork base.

2 Wind line on to the reel until the float is hanging four to five feet below the rod tip – the perfect position for casting.

3 Assuming you're right-handed (reverse the directions if you're left-handed), hook the line near the roller on the bail arm with the first finger of your right hand.

4 Gripping the line against the butt of the rod, open the bail arm on the reel so that line is primed to peel off the spool. Your finger pulling the line tight will stop it releasing.

5 Swing the plummet over your right shoulder and hold the rod with its tip angled slightly behind you and its lower end in front of the centre of your face.

6 Line up the rod with the place you want to cast to. Pick a permanent far bank marker such as a tree or a fishing platform – don't pick something that will move!

7 In a smooth sweeping motion, push forward with your right hand and pull in with your left hand – this tensions the line and propels the float and plummet forwards. The weight of the plummet will pull line off the reel and the float will follow the path of the weight. With practice you'll be able to land the plummet and float exactly in the area where you want to measure the depth and fish.

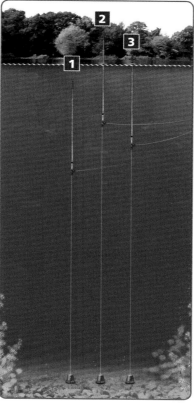

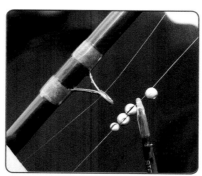

10 Mark the position of the float adaptor on the rod with white correction fluid or a white chinagraph pencil. This record of the water depth means you can alter your rig through the day to fish at any specific depth you wish and can always return the rig to the exact depth of the swim without having to re-plumb.

This ability to set a rig to the exact depth quickly is also useful if your line snaps or becomes badly tangled and you have to set up a new rig – it's a simple task to tie the same rig as before and use the measuring guide marked on the rod to set the depth.

8 It's always worth taking time to plumb the depth of a swim properly, so make this process something that you do every time you go float fishing.

The heavy plummet will plunge to the bottom of the lake. If the float is set at less than the depth of the water it will be instantly pulled under the surface (position 1). If so you need to retrieve the rig, slide the locking shot and float up the line further from the hook, and then re-cast.

If it's set too deep the under-shotted float will ride very high in the water (position 2). If so you need to bring the rig back in and slide the float and shot down the line, nearer to the hook.

After a few re-casts and adjustments to the float's position you'll eventually end up with the float sitting perfectly on the surface with around 1cm of the tip poking above the water (position 3). The rig is now set at the precise depth of the water (called 'dead-depth').

9 Bring the float in, remove the plummet, and carefully slide the hook on to the front of the reel seat or the hook retaining ring if your rod has one. Wind line on to the reel until it's pulled tight, then hold the float against the rod.

Ready to fish!

Now that the depth has been established and marked on your rod you just have to fine-tune the shotting of the rig and you're ready to get fishing.

Over the page are three diagrams showing where you place your split shot and what components you use to construct a great fish-catching float rig.

3 essential waggler rigs

The three detailed waggler rig diagrams shown here cover 90% of the stillwater float situations that you'll face. Two are for angling on the lake bed and one is for angling high in the water column – often called 'on-the-drop fishing', as the aim of the set-up is to get your bait taken by fish as it slowly sinks through the water.

Remember that when we plumbed the depth we used a float that was purposely under-shotted by around 1AAA. Now's the time to add this missing weight to dot the float down in the water and make it ready to fish with.

These three diagrams show you where and how much shot needs to be added to the line. Use these graphics as a guide and you won't go far wrong.

In the construction of each of these rigs the four golden rules of waggler fishing outlined on pages 34/35 have been followed, so they're unlikely to tangle and should catch you plenty of fish.

Over the next pages we'll provide details of how to cast a float, bait the hook, feed the swim to get fish there; and then comes the exciting bit – actually catching a fish!

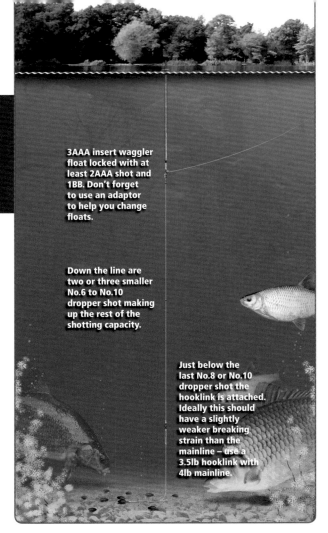

3AAA insert waggler float locked with at least 2AAA shot and 1BB. Don't forget to use an adaptor to help you change floats.

Down the line are two or three smaller No.6 to No.10 dropper shot making up the rest of the shotting capacity.

Just below the last No.8 or No.10 dropper shot the hooklink is attached. Ideally this should have a slightly weaker breaking strain than the mainline – use a 3.5lb hooklink with 4lb mainline.

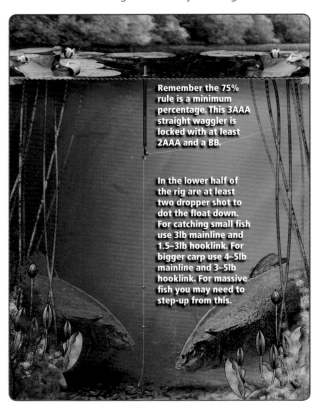

Remember the 75% rule is a minimum percentage. This 3AAA straight waggler is locked with at least 2AAA and a BB.

In the lower half of the rig are at least two dropper shot to dot the float down. For catching small fish use 3lb mainline and 1.5–3lb hooklink. For bigger carp use 4–5lb mainline and 3–5lb hooklink. For massive fish you may need to step-up from this.

This is an up-in-the-water rig to catch fish in the upper layers. As long as you've followed the golden rules of waggler fishing it shouldn't tangle in flight.

Catapult some maggots first then quickly cast into the baited area.

Your hookbait drops alongside the falling free offerings and fish take it as it falls. As with the other rigs on this page the hooklink and mainline are balanced to the size of fish you're catching.

Casting and sinking the line

Launching a float into the water – known as casting – is something plenty of anglers have a hard time with. The commonest problems are repeated tangles on the reel, line and float, and being unable to control the flight of the rig so that it lands in the same place every time.

The guide to plumbing on pages 38/39 gave you a step-by-step guide to casting which can be used in exactly the same way when a baited float rig is being launched without a plummet. However, once you've cast out a baited rig you must then sink the line to ensure that the float stays in the position you've cast it and isn't dragged out of position by the wind.

Here are two methods of sinking the line.

The simple way to sink the line

1 When the float lands on the surface, close the bail arm and turn the reel handle a couple of times to tighten the line.

2 Plunge the end two or three feet of the rod into the water at a 30° angle and quickly wind the handle two or three turns. The float will dip under and the line will be sunk. Repeat this procedure until all the mainline is sunk.

3 Angle the rod clear of the water and let it sit on a rod rest head. Using a rod rest will make your fishing far more comfortable.

The advanced way to sink your line

1 After casting, tighten the line by dipping the tip of the rod beneath the water and turning the reel handle until the float twitches.

2 After tightening the line the top two to three feet of the rod should be kept underwater.

3 Whip the rod upwards until it clears the water. This drags the line below the surface tension and quickly sinks it.

Picking a bait

So that's the rig perfectly set up to catch fish. All we need to do now is look at baits to put on your hook, and ways to introduce extra food into the area you're fishing in order to attract fish.

Feeding on the float

Feeding your swim to catch more

Imagine you're feeling a bit hungry and go looking for something to eat. If there's just one chip lying somewhere in the house it'll be difficult to find – in fact you're likely to give up looking and go somewhere else. But now imagine that in the kitchen a roast dinner has been cooked and laid out on a plate, filling the air with tempting aromas. You'd go straight to the plate and tuck in!

Apply this same scenario to fishing and it's instantly obvious why you scatter extra items of food in the area you're fishing – to attract more fish there and get them feeding. Called loosefeed, free offerings or freebies, these extra baits are thrown or catapulted into the area around your float, and this is one of the most important disciplines you must learn.

The best anglers all feed free offerings with great accuracy and regularity: as four-times World Champion Bob Nudd has repeatedly told me, 'Fishing is all about feeding.' His comment stresses how important it is to regularly feed a swim, because this essential inducement draws fish to the bait on your hook and stimulates their appetite enough to eat it.

It's impossible to recommend a definitive quantity and timescale regarding how much and how often you should loosefeed – fishing is governed by variable conditions that affect how strongly fish feed and how much food you

Above: Daiwa star Will Raison fires maggots at his float. Regular and accurate catapulting of free offerings is essential to draw fish to your hookbait.

should inject into your swim. The weather, the number of fish in a fishery and how hungry they may be are just some of the factors that affect loosefeeding.

That said, the sequence below demonstrates how to use a catapult to fire free offerings close to your float. It also suggests a couple of different feeding patterns that have proved successful.

1 There are dozens of catapults on the market capable of firing different baits to different distances. Some feature fine elastic and tiny pouches for feeding at very short range on narrow canals. Others feature thick, powerful elastic that launches baits a long way. For float fishing a medium-rated catty is ideal.

2 The distance you cast your float should be influenced by how far you can accurately loosefeed. There's no point launching your float way beyond the range of your free offerings, as your hookbait will sit in splendid isolation and you won't attract fish to eat it. If you're using maggots or casters you'll struggle to catapult them accurately beyond 20 or 25m. The picture shows former world champion and all-round great angler Tom Pickering in action.

3 Don't overfill your catapult pouch with bait. A standard feeding routine that's stood the test of time is called 'little and often'. As it implies, you load just a pinch of maggots or casters into the pouch. The key word here is 'pinch' – a pinch of bait is basically 10 to 20 maggots or casters.

4 Hold the frame of the catapult in your left hand and the tag on the bottom of the pouch in your right (reverse this if you're left-handed).

5 Pushing your left arm out and locking your elbow, push the frame of the catapult away from you and pull back slightly on the elastic to tension it ready for firing.

6 Release the pouch and fire the baits at the float. Practice will perfect how hard you need to pull back the elastic to get the bait near the float. It's essential the float and bait go in the same place every cast so that the bait builds up and creates an area of concentrated feeding activity. Getting the loosefeed near your float is therefore a vital skill that will catch you more fish.

When to feed...

The 'often' part of the 'little and often' feeding pattern will vary according to circumstances. However, as a starting point you won't go far wrong if you feed 10 to 20 baits every one to two minutes during the warmer months, or every five minutes during winter. If the fish are feeding well you may need to step up the quantity of loosefeed, feeding 40 or 50 baits every minute or two for example. Just remember to keep picking up the catapult – one of the main reasons why anglers don't catch as many fish as they should is that they forget (or are too lazy!) to keep feeding.

Many anglers get stuck in a rut of poor feeding. They may blast a pouchful of bait loosely in the direction of the float every half-hour then wonder why they don't catch anything.

Put simply, they aren't introducing enough bait and consequently aren't attracting fish by the sight and sound of feed frequently hitting and sinking through the water.

You've got a bite...strike!!

You now have a great rig, baits to go on the hook, and you understand the need to provide additional food near the float on a regular basis.

But what happens when you get a bite? How do you hook and play a fish?

Turn the page and find out…

Striking and landing fish

With your float cast out and loosefeed attracting fish to your hookbait it won't take long to earn a bite.

If you've got your float dotted down so that just a small portion of the tip sticks above the surface it will be very sensitive to fish mouthing the bait – the merest tug on the line will pull the float under the water. In angling parlance this is a 'guzunder' bite and you should strike by making a swift vertical lift of the rod.

The strike comes from the elbow, not the shoulder, and speed is the key more than brute force – you're looking to jab the hook home, not hammer it.

If you've sunk your line properly, and have kept it tight between the rod and float, a quick vertical strike will pull the line and connect with the fish feeding on your hookbait. The rod will bend and act as a shock absorber.

The other type of bite to look for is a 'lift bite'. This gets its name from the fact that the float doesn't go under, it actually rises in the water. This is caused by a fish intercepting the bait as it sinks or else picking it up and swimming upwards in the water column. The weight of the split shot is held up by the fish rather than pulling on the float, and with less shot pulling down on the float the tip lifts and the angler gets a bite which is almost as obvious as the float pulling under … strike!

If the fish is a small one winding it slowly in and swinging it to hand is an easy process. But if you get lucky and hook a larger fish that tries to run away from you, then you need to release line from the reel to prevent it breaking the nylon or pulling the hook out. There are two ways of doing this.

The easier is to flick the anti-reverse switch found on every reel. This allows the bail arm to rotate backwards, so that if you turn the handle in reverse line will go out

Below: A swift upward strike will set the hook, then a smooth pumping action should allow you to regain line on to your reel, which will bring the fish close to the bank for netting.

rather than come in, and the fish can expend some of its energy by running away from you.

The other way of allowing a fish to run is by using the drag or clutch system. As mentioned earlier in this chapter a good reel will have a reliable drag system. This tensioning device allows you to dial in more or less resistance to a running fish. If you've got it set up correctly, then before the fish nears the breaking strain of the line the clutch will slip and release line from the spool.

Depending on the size, power and stamina of a hooked fish you may need to release line several times before it starts to run out of steam. You can then coax it towards the bank with a pumping motion – you gain line on the fish by pulling back on the rod to ease the fish towards you then wrap the line you've gained on to the reel as you lower the rod again. If you're patient the fish will soon be brought within the reach of a landing net and pole and you can coax it into the mesh.

Congratulations! With a bit of luck you've just caught a personal best fish!

Left: Bigger fish may force you to give line using the drag system. Make sure you set yours so that line will pull off the reel under mild tension.

Below: Get it right, as European Champion angler Steve Hemingray has done here, and you can get a big bag of large fish on the float.

Waggler float fishing tips

Interchangeable tips

Many insert waggler floats allow you to alter the colour of the tip to make it easier to see in different light conditions. Buy the right float and a pack of tips and you'll be able to see your float when other anglers are struggling to spot theirs. You'll also be able to swap tips to suit the prevailing wind conditions.

Feather the cast

Once you're well practised at casting a float try dabbing your finger on the line just before the float lands on the water. Called 'feathering the line', this slows down the final stage of the float's flight, which helps to ensure that the line is strung when it hits the water. This virtually eliminates any chance of a tangle.

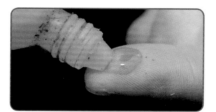

Line up your shot

When placing a bulk of large shot near the float, or a few small droppers close together down the line, ensure that the splits in the shot all line up. This helps to create a neat barrel shape in the shot that improves the flight and casting distance of a float.

Clean your line

Sinking your line is important when float fishing, but sometimes the nylon gets smeared in greasy residue that collects on the surface of the water. This can stop the line sinking.

To combat this, carry a tiny bottle containing a 50:50 blend of washing up liquid and water. Cast out your float, dab a spot of the solution on your fingers and then wind the line back between them. The oil is removed and the line will sink.

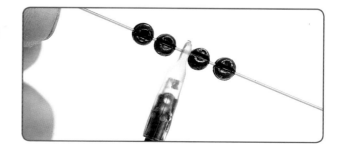

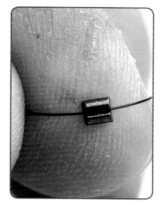
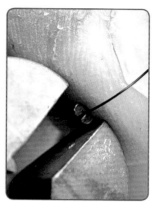
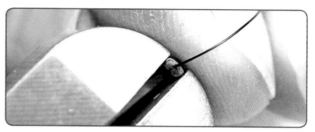

Having trouble with small shot?

Some anglers struggle to pinch very small round shot on the line, and many people find these cylindrical Stotz shot from Preston Innovations easier to use. They're applied to the line using a pair of mini-pliers called a Stotta. Just put the line in the split and use the Stotta to squeeze the Stotz on to it. They don't damage the line, and the Stotta tool can also be used to remove them.

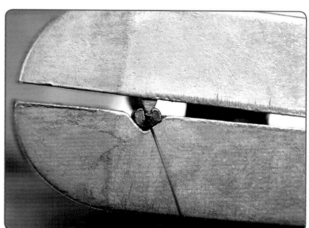

Fish with the wind behind you

Casting a lightweight float into a head-on wind is difficult, as is casting across a side wind. It's far easier to be accurate with your cast if you fish with the breeze coming over your shoulder from behind you – the float flies straighter and is less likely to get dragged out of position.

Want some advice about advanced float fishing?

This section has supplied you with a grounding in the key stillwater float fishing skills, but one of the strengths of the float is that it's versatile enough to be used in different situations. Next we'll provide you with details of two distinct styles of advanced float fishing – the pellet waggler for fishing in lakes, and the stick float for rivers.

The pellet waggler

Think of this as waggler fishing on steroids.

Using a big, fat float attached to the line with a special connector weight, this tactic is designed to be used with a power float rod when trying to catch big carp in the summer months, when warmer temperatures encourage them to feed in the mid to upper layers. The diagram and step-by-step pictures show you how top Maver-sponsored angler and former England youth international and under-22 World Champion Callum Dicks constructs this beefy set-up.

This is an extreme tactic that contradicts some of the general principles we established earlier, but because you're angling for much bigger fish you need to use much stronger line, and the No.8 rule is ignored because this is a huge float that works because of its sheer size.

Rather than dotting it right down you leave a large part of the hugely buoyant float standing proud of the surface, and when a greedy carp snatches the pellet hookbait it pulls the line tight to the float and instantly hooks itself as a result of the resistance the float offers.

This is a carp-only tactic that should be used in high summer.

1 Setting up Callum's pellet waggler rig is easy. A rubber float stop is slid on to the reel line first followed by a Steve Mayo pellet waggler attachment holding a 4SSG Maver Foam pellet waggler. These super buoyant floats are made of foam to stop them diving under the water when they land. A BB shot is pinched below the float, and the hooklink is attached below that.

2 The Mayo attachment device is a heavy drilled weight that has a large hole in one side. This slips over the BB shot.

3 The float is then locked by sliding the float stop down to the top of the weight.

4 The hooklink is 460mm (18in) long and made of 0.18mm (7lb) Maver Genesis line. Below that is a size 14 Maver Series 3 hook knotted to the hooklink with an elastic bait band in the loop. The band is pinched against the side of an 8mm hard feed pellet.

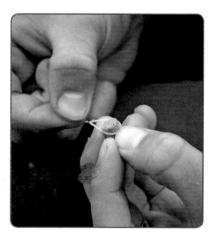

5 The band is stretched over the pellet and then the tension is released.

6 The band contracts and grips the bait tightly.

7 With his baited rig ready to cast, Callum drops the float in the water at his feet, picks up his catapult and grabs a pinch of pellets.

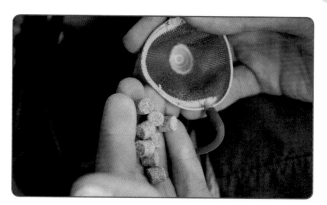

8 You don't need lots of bait, just regular helpings – six to eight pellets every 30 seconds is about right. Callum fires this payload into the area he's going to cast.

9 The rule is simple – if your catapult is lying untouched for a minute or two you're either busy landing a fish or you're not feeding enough.

10 As pellets hit the water his catapult is already down and Callum is casting out the baited rig. The quicker you are the better, as you want the hookbait to sink with the freebies.

11 As the float lands in the loosefed area Callum tightens the line to the float and watches for a bite. The foam float instantly sits up in the water – bites often come within seconds as carp ambush the falling freebies and hookbait.

12 If nothing happens in 20 seconds Callum twitches the float hard to make the float bob under and the hookbait 'jump' in the water. He quickly tightens the line and fires out another payload of pellets.

13 If there's no response after another 15–20 seconds he winds in and returns to step 8. Once the fish have started coming to the regular loosefeeding this is what will start happening – you'll be bagging up!

14 Using an 11ft Maver Powerlite two-piece rod Callum gained the upper hand on this Larford mirror. Note the float hanging 60cm above the carp's head.

15 Different sizes of Mayo pellet waggler attachments are available for different-sized floats. By reducing the number of split shot pinched on the line to just one they cut the risk of damaging the line and causing it to snap.

16 Proof of the pudding – a Larford Lakes mirror that fell for the pellet waggler. It was caught 60cm deep in around 3.5m of water.

This diagram shows how the pellet waggler works.

First the pellets go in (1), making distinct splashes.

The float follows (2), making another splash to alert carp that 'dinner is served'!

To withstand the strain of catching big carp Callum ties a 60cm length of 12lb line to the end of his 8lb reel line (3).

This buffer of strong line is called a shock leader and makes the rig more robust, the BB shot inside the Mayo attachment is less likely to damage 12lb line than 8lb line.

Reacting to the sound of loosefeed and the float, carp rise to intercept the falling freebies. If you get your hookbait among the loosefeed you'll catch fish (4).

The stick float

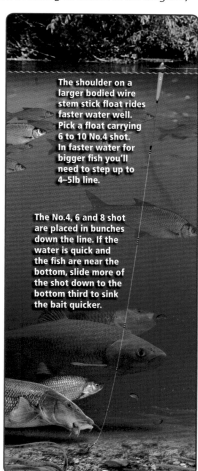

Fishing a float in a river requires a number of fundamental changes to be made to the general principles we've demonstrated with the waggler float.

The most obvious difference between these two styles of float fishing concerns the shape and construction of the floats themselves and the way they're attached to the line.

Unlike a waggler, which is attached to the line at the bottom end only, a stick float is attached at both ends of the float. Silicone rubber sleeves are used to trap the reel line against the float so as to fix it in place. This enables the float to be run (or 'trotted') down a river without it being sucked under by the current. The fact that the line exits from the top of the float rather than the base means that it can be held up against the flow as you allow it to trot downstream.

To give you better control of the float it's also essential that you use a floating reel line – speak to your tackle dealer to find a line that floats, or buy a can of line floatant, a special aerosol that can be sprayed on to the line, covering it in an oily film that makes it float.

Another major difference with the way stick float rigs are set up is that the shotting patterns are completely different. Forget all about the four golden waggler rules detailed earlier. Instead of the shot being bulked at the base of the float, when you set up a stick float rig you either spread the weight down the entire length of the rig or you place the bulk of the shot in the bottom third.

The aim of a stick float rig is to combat the flow of a river, to get the hookbait down to the riverbed quickly and to keep it there.

A classic shotting pattern for a straight stick float is shown in the diagram below left. Commonly called the 'shirt-button pattern' because of the way the shot is evenly spaced down the entire length of the rig, this very slender float is suited to fishing in slow to medium-paced rivers that trundle along at a ponderous walking pace with a smooth current. The spread-out shot allows the hookbait to drop to the riverbed in a smooth arc.

Once again the shotting capacity is marked on the side of the float, the loading often being stated in terms of the quantity of No.4 shot the float will carry. As a general guide attach the equivalent of one No.4 shot for every foot of water of the swim you're fishing – for example, use a six No.4 float for a 6ft-deep swim.

Another popular pattern of shotting is to bunch the shot in the bottom half of the rig as shown in the diagram, which depicts a typical wire-stemmed stick float. This design of stick float features a fatter body than the straight stick. It also has a pronounced shoulder on the top of the float, which gives the wire stem more buoyancy so that it can be used in medium- to fast-paced rivers without getting sucked under the water.

The wire used for the stem also gives it more weight and solidity. This stabilises the float and makes it suitable for faster water that would swamp a straight stick.

A 6x4 straight stick float is ideal for most slow to medium paced rivers. It is fixed with three silicone rubber sleeves, one on the top of the float and two on the stem.

The shirt button shotting sees evenly spaced No.6, 8 and 10 shot spread down the line. 3lb nylon is usually sufficient for maggots or for caster fishing a size 16-20 hook is ideal.

The shoulder on a larger bodied wire stem stick float rides faster water well. Pick a float carrying 6 to 10 No.4 shot. In faster water for bigger fish you'll need to step up to 4–5lb line.

The No.4, 6 and 8 shot are placed in bunches down the line. If the water is quick and the fish are near the bottom, slide more of the shot down to the bottom third to sink the bait quicker.

Casting and trotting a stick float the Tom Pickering way

1 Stand side-on to the point in the river that you want to target, with the rod held in your right hand. Open the bail arm on the reel, trap the line against the spool with your first finger and hold the hooklink in your other hand.

2 Hold the hooklink 25cm (10in) above the bait to prevent tangles and to avoid hooking yourself when you cast out.

3 Holding the hooklink tightly, pull the rod away from you to tension the rig and bend the rod.

4 Sweep the rod towards the river in an arc at the same time as you release the hooklink. Follow through the flight of the float and release the line held near the reel. Feather the line pouring off the open spool just before the rig hits the water.

5 The result should be that the line avoids tangling as the rig is strung out when it hits the water. This picture shows a shirt-button shotting pattern hitting the water – you can see each shot landing followed by the final splash which is the hookbait.

6 Once the rig is in the water flick the line tight behind the float (this is called 'mending the line') and tease line off the open reel spool with your fingers. This will allow the float to trot downstream with the current.

7 Remember to keep feeding – because the river is flowing your free offerings will be quickly washed away.

8 On every trot the float must be accompanied by free offerings identical to the hookbait.

9 Get it right and you'll catch fish like this skimmer bream, landed by top flight angler Tom Pickering.

Combating fast water

For fishing in really fast and turbulent rivers, the diagram below shows the ideal bulk shotting pattern to combat this type of water using a loafer or chubber float. These extra-buoyant floats are made from balsa or plastic, and for this set-up a bulk of larger split shot (usually SSGs, AAAs and BBs) is placed in the bottom third of the rig. This hefty loading bombs the hookbait to the riverbed and keeps it there, even if the swirling current is trying to lift the bait.

The additional buoyancy of this type of float means that it's ideal for use with larger, heavier baits like luncheon meat, pellets or large lumps of bread when fishing for specimen chub and barbel.

As with the pellet waggler, you beef up the rod, line and hook, especially if you're fishing where large chub and barbel may be hooked. Not only does the weight and fight of the fish strain your tackle but the push of the current adds extra stress. It's not unusual to use 5lb reel line and size 10 to 16 heavy wire hooks when fishing these venues.

Whereas a 12ft or 13ft rod is ideal for waggler fishing, when you're trotting a float down a river a 14ft or 15ft rod allows you to mend the line better and keep it tight to the float.

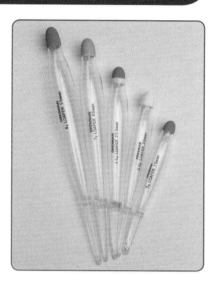

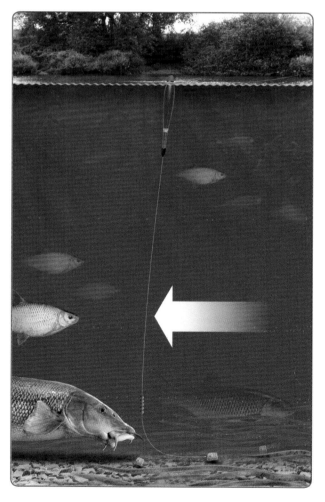

Easily hooked

Learning to tie a spade end hook is an essential angling skill but it is one that lots of anglers struggle with due to the size of the hook and the fiddly knot.

As a general rule spade end hooks are available in smaller sizes and they're made of finer, lighter wire than the majority of eyed hook patterns.

This means the ability to tie and use spade end hooks massively aids your fishing performance as you can create more delicate rigs that are better when times are tough or you're fishing for smaller species like roach and skimmer bream.

Follow these step-by-step instructions and you'll soon be tying knots like a professional…

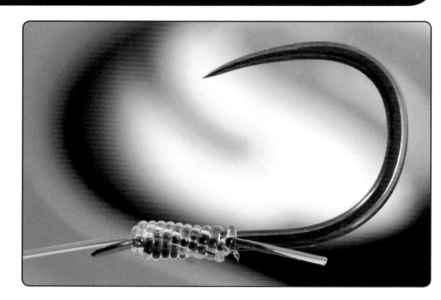

1 I use a Drennan Hook Tyer (the maroon coloured one) to tie my spade end hooks. It creates a perfect finish every time.

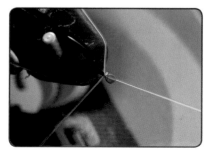

2 Clamp the hook in the jaws ensuring the front of the spade faces towards the metal lever.

3 I hold the tyer in my left hand and thread the line around the lever in an anti-clockwise fashion.

4 I'll trap the line against the tyer in my left hand and pass the end of the line (tag) underneath the other piece of line.

5 Make one anti-clockwise revolution of the hook tyer and ensure the line sits as shown, butting up against the spade.

6 Once you have this crucial part correct, continue to rotate the hook tyer anti-clockwise to form the rest of the turns (12 in total).

7 Loop the tag end of the line (the part in your right hand) over the gold pin on the hook tyer.

8 Hold everything tight and push the metal lever forward with your left thumb.

9 The line will loop off the metal lever as shown. Make sure you still hold everything tight.

10 Pull the main part of the line (not the tag) and the loop will begin to close.

11 Keep pulling the main part of the line until it closes the knot at the base of the whipping.

12 The tag of line will still be around the gold pin.

13 Pull back the metal lever to release the hook from the jaws. Ensure the line is around the gold pin as you do this.

14 The gold pin will pull the line back through the whipping loop you have created to finish the knot.

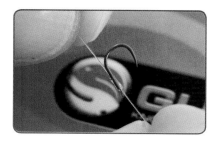

15 Now gently pull tight between thumb and forefinger on each hand and hold for several seconds so the knot can 'bed down' properly.

16 I now place the hook around the gold pin and pull the main part of the line to fully secure the whipping.

17 Once you're happy trim the tag part of line. I always leave between 2mm and 3mm of tag to safeguard against any slippage under extreme loads.

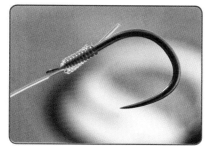

18 The perfect finished article! Neat, strong and ready to help you catch more fish.

Baiting your hook

There are literally hundreds of different kinds and combinations of baits you can put on your hook to catch fish. Throughout each chapter of this book we'll detail a selection that are particularly relevant to the style of fishing being discussed. However, the baits listed in Chapters 2, 3 and 4 (float, swimfeeder and pole fishing) are all interchangeable between the different disciplines. We'll start by looking at the natural baits that are often used when float fishing.

How to hook maggots

Maggots are the larvae of the bluebottle fly and are one of the most popular baits. Here's how to hook them:

1 Use a medium to fine wire hook in size 16, 18 or 20. Offer the blunt end of the maggot to the hook point.

2 Nick the hook through a sliver of skin – the idea is to avoid bursting the maggot, as it will remain lively and look more attractive to a fish.

3 This is how *not* to do it. The hook has been buried deep into the maggot and roughly poked out of the other side; this has burst the grub and it will soon be an ex-maggot. It will stop wriggling and no self-respecting fish will go near it.

4 Two maggots can be hooked through the blunt end side-by-side. Double maggot hookbaits can make use of different colours of bait – a red and a white maggot, for example.

5 Another way to hook two maggots is like this – one through the blunt end, the other nicked through the narrow end. This stops the bait acting like a propeller as you retrieve it, which can twist and tangle the line.

6 For shy-biting fish that are giving you bites but you can't hook them, try this. Slide the hook into the blunt end and carefully tease it out of the side of the bait.

How to hook casters

Casters are the chrysalis stage of a maggot before it turns into a fly. The crunchy shell of the bait is hugely attractive to most coarse fish, especially roach, carp, tench and bream, but because they're more delicate than a rubbery-skinned maggot many anglers struggle to hook them. This is how you should do it:

1 There are two ways to present casters: you can either leave the hook point showing if the fish are biting boldly, or you can hide it inside the crunchy shell if the fish are feeding cautiously.

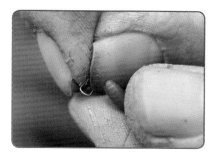

2 To leave the point exposed pick a size 16 or 18 razor sharp medium to fine wire hook.

3 Push the point into the side of the caster just below its blunt end.

4 Turn the hook to slide the bend through the bait and poke the point out of its top.

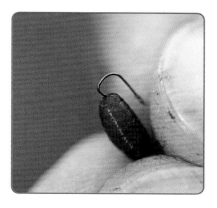

5 To bury the hook inside the caster spear the point into the middle of its blunt end.

6 Carefully rotate the hook to sink the entire point and bend inside the shell of the bait.

7 Tap the spade end of the hook where the line is attached to it. This buries the entire hook inside the bait.

8 For a double caster, hook the first bait through the blunt end and out of the side, then hook the second caster in the side and tease the point out through the top.

Chopped worms

Tench, bream, chub, roach, perch and carp are just some of the fish species that love worms. A natural bait loaded with rich juices and which wriggles like fury, worms are a great bait that can get a bite when all other baits are failing miserably. Here's what to do with them:

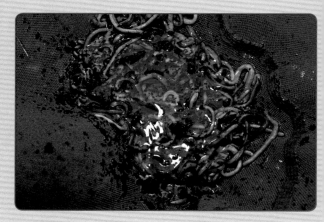

1 Take a handful of worms (most tackle shops sell dendrobaenas in large bags), drop them in a fine mesh landing net or riddle and dunk them in water.

2 Wash the soil off the worms to clean them and make it easier to cut them up.

3 Get busy with some scissors to reduce the worms into tiny chunks measuring around half a centimetre.

4 Add a palmful of casters to the mess of chopped worms leaking their juices out of the cut ends.

5 A blend of minced worms and fresh casters is the perfect mix for pole cupping or potting (see Chapter 4). A pinch of this mixture can be sandwiched between groundbait if you use a feeder (see Chapter 3).

How to hook worms

One of the strengths of worm fishing is that you can vary how you present your hookbait. Here are some suggestions, whether you're using a small bait for quality roach or a 'snake' for big tench, perch or chub.

1 Lobworms are brilliant big fish baits. Slide a size 6 to 10 hook through the slightly tougher 'saddle' band round the bait.

2 Poke the point out of the saddle. If you're using a barbless hook spear a tiny piece of elastic band on to the hook and slide it down to the worm. This grips the hook and stops a Houdini worm escaping!

3 A great 'cocktail' bait is a large chunk of lobworm locked to the hook with a red maggot. Early-season tench love this combo.

4 While big lobworms can tempt specimen chub, perch or tench, an inch-long chunk is often better than a whole bait as it pumps out more smell.

5 If you're fishing in lakes for large roach and perch, a chunk of redworm or dendrobaena worm is usually better than a 'snake' of bait.

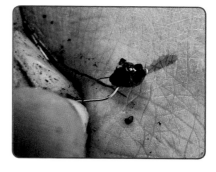

6 On heavily fished lakes where fish are used to seeing chopped worms, using tiny pieces on a size 20 hook can get you extra bites.

7 These mini worm snacks can be half the size of a caster but they're brilliant for shy-biting roach during colder months.

8 Threading a section of worm round the bend of a hook to cover the shank can be another useful way to trick educated fish.

9 Tipping a half-worm with a caster is an excellent hookbait when feeder fishing with groundbait for bream.

CHAPTER 3 Coarse Fishing Manual

SWIMFEEDER FISHING

Essential kit for swimfeeder fishing   64

Kit extras that'll get you geared up   68

The open-end feeder explained   70

Making groundbait   72

The block-end feeder explained   74

The flatbed method feeder explained   76

The method feeder explained   79

The time-bomb river feeder explained   82

The pellet feeder explained   86

How to cast a feeder   94

Setting up your seat box or chair   96

Legering   98

Hookbaits for feeders   102

Get the best from your feeder fishing   105

Swimfeeder fishing is the bigger, rougher, tougher and noisier brother to quiet little float fishing! Whereas a float is a delicate tool to tease a bite from an unsuspecting fish, modern swimfeeder techniques are much bolder and usually succeed *because* of their in-your-face approach, not despite it.

Swimfeeders (a term often shortened to 'feeders') come in a host of different shapes and sizes. However, although there are some significant differences in how they perform their job there's one fundamental similarity between all of them: put simply, they're either stuffed or coated with bait before they're cast into the water.

Like floats, different feeders can be used to cope with both still waters and rivers, but where the big difference lies is that you don't need to loosefeed the area a swimfeeder is cast into. The very principle underpinning how and why a feeder catches fish is that it carries its own payload of free offerings. Once cast into the water the feed washes out or off the feeder; this attracts fish to the area, where they soon find your hookbait lying nearby, and the rest is history!

As the fish feed on the freebies they gain confidence in the banquet spilling out of the feeder, and your hookbait just becomes another part of the feast – the result is that you catch plenty of fish.

One of the other key characteristics of feeder fishing is that you can usually cast the baited rig much further than you can launch a float. The weight of a feeder packed with bait allows the angler to generate much more casting power, and a good rod, reel and line combination can propel a feeder rig 30m, 40m or even 50m with relative ease.

This means the feeder is more suited to searching a fishery, as you can cast to areas that are simply out of normal float and loosefeed range. What's more, the extra weight of a feeder means that it sinks rapidly to the bottom and stays there. This makes it particularly useful for combating a flowing river and for stillwater fishing when a gale-force wind is moving the water and buffeting a lighter float rig.

In boxing terms a loaded swimfeeder is a heavyweight compared to a waggler float in the lightweight division!

But there's one more significant difference between feeder fishing techniques and those employed with the float: how you register a bite. With a float you sit and watch the coloured tip dotted down in the water; when it goes under or dramatically lifts you've got a bite and strike. But when you've cast a swimfeeder 40m to sit on the bottom of a lake or river you need a different way to resister bites from fish. This is where the slender top section of the special rod used for feeder fishing comes into play.

Called a quivertip, this superfine and responsive top section of the rod twitches, pulls round or springs back when a fish picks up your hookbait and pulls on the reel line. Just as a float going under the water prompts you to strike so the movement of the quivertip does the same job. Clearly, therefore, the rod you choose for feeder fishing has a central role in the technique as it's not just responsible for casting the feeder but is also the equipment through which the bite is registered.

Without further ado lets look at the special kit you need for fishing with a swimfeeder.

Essential kit for swimfeeder fishing

The rod you pick for swimfeeder fishing has to perform two starkly contrasting jobs. On the one hand it has to be powerful enough to cast a heavy, loaded swimfeeder a long way – this means it has to have considerable inherent strength and stiffness so that it can generate the required power; while on the other it needs to maintain suppleness and subtlety – if the quivertip end section is going to be effective at showing a bite by a fish picking up your bait 30 or 40m away it must bend easily enough to show the fish's interest.

Just think about how opposed these two demands are. It has to be strong and powerful for casting but soft and sensitive for bite detection, so it's not hard to see why you need to choose your feeder rod carefully and why it's a job for a specialist piece of kit that's been carefully made for the task.

Thankfully there are now dozens of good and affordable feeder fishing rods on the market, and you just need the help of a good tackle dealer to help you pick the right one.

The first thing to realise is that one feeder rod is not the same as another. Different models have been designed with a variety of tasks in mind and as a general principle feeder rods can be split into three camps – light, medium and heavy action.

Light feeder rods are usually 8–10ft long, they don't have a very stiff bottom section, and they're supplied with a selection of soft quivertips sporting 0.25oz to 1.5oz test curve ratings (see guide over the page for information on quivertip strength). These rods are made for casting tiny feeders that don't hold much bait and don't weigh very much. They're used on small lakes, ponds and narrow canals where smaller fish are the main quarry.

Stepping up to a medium feeder rod, this is usually 10–12ft long but boasts a thicker, stiffer butt and middle section which gives it significantly more casting power. The range of quivertips supplied with the rod will be stiffer and stronger too. Usually they'll have a test curve of 1oz to 3oz to cope with the rigours of casting a heavier feeder longer distances. Rods like this can cope with casting larger, heavier feeders that carry more bait, and allow you to propel such feeders a good distance. They're usually used for fishing reasonably-sized lakes and small or slow-moving rivers.

Then we step up to the daddy of the feeder world, the heavy feeder rod, used for launching big and heavy swimfeeders a long way. Usually 12–14ft long, these rods sport a much thicker middle and butt section to give the rod

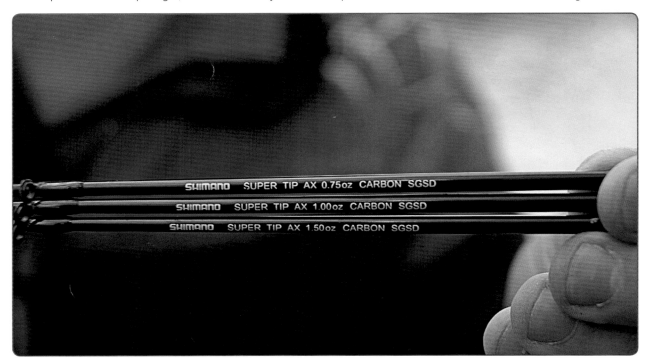

SHIMANO SUPER TIP AX 0.75oz CARBON SGSD

SHIMANO SUPER TIP AX 1.00oz CARBON SGSD

SHIMANO SUPER TIP AX 1.50oz CARBON SGSD

immense casting power. They're supplied with beefier quivertips of 3oz to 6oz, and are generally used for extreme-range fishing on lakes or for fishing big, powerful rivers where you need a large, heavy feeder to anchor the bait on the riverbed and stop it getting washed away.

In this chapter we'll provide details of a number of modern feeder rigs for fishing in both still waters and rivers, since depending on your tactics and the type of venue being fished different types of feeder rod will be better suited to different situations. However, in the majority of modern, managed fisheries light feeder rods are rarely used, since unless you fish regularly on very small fisheries for little fish they can be considered something of a luxury.

The only real exception to this general rule would be when it comes to winter angling for fish that are reluctant to feed in bitterly cold conditions. In this extreme case, using a very small feeder carrying a pinch of bait can get you a tentative bite that shows up best on a super-sensitive quivertip.

Of much more general use to the vast majority of anglers is the medium feeder rod, as they can more than meet the casting demands of most anglers fishing on the bulk of still waters and even a large number of rivers. The range of quivertips is also sensitive enough to register the vast majority of bites.

Look for a rod that's around 11ft long and made entirely of carbon rather than glass or a composite of the two. Some rods have the flexibility to be used at different lengths, such as 9ft and 11 ft or 10ft and 12ft. This can prove beneficial, as the shorter rod can be used in cramped swims whereas the longer rod tends to have better casting performance if the fish are some distance away.

To echo the advice already offered in the float fishing section, don't automatically choose the cheapest rod, and seek the honest advice of a good tackle dealer. Some very cheap rods can lack the backbone to cast a loaded feeder accurately and you must also remember that repeated casting with a loaded feeder puts tremendous strain on a rod. If you skimp on the kit you buy don't be surprised if it lets you down.

Finally, it must be said that an increasing number of extreme feeder fishing situations demand that you step up to a heavy feeder rod. Later in the chapter we'll detail tactics that may be suitable for this most beefy of feeder rods; if you're likely to use these techniques then a heavy swimfeeder rod may be required.

In general, though, you can get a very good medium feeder rod that's versatile enough to cover the majority of fishing situations. Buy wisely, don't skimp on quality, and you should get years of good service out of your rod.

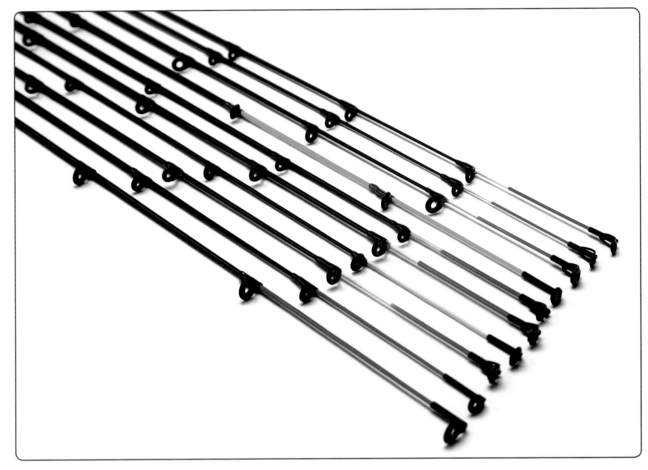

Quivertips explained

One of the most vital pieces of equipment used for feeder fishing is the quivertip – after all, it's the thing that tells you when you've got a bite.

Fitted into the end of the rod, either as an integral piece of it or more often as a plug-in section, the quivertip is supposed to be fine enough to show a bite but strong enough to cope with the demands of casting a laden swimfeeder. If you get the choice of quivertip wrong and use one that's far too strong and stiff for the species you're trying the catch it can cost you fish. For example, shy-biting species like roach will often feel the resistance offered by a very stiff 5oz tip as soon as they pick up the bait, and they'll instantly spit it out because they know there's something suspicious about it.

By contrast if you use a very soft

0.5oz quivertip when you try to cast a heavy feeder a long way you're heading for disaster – this superfine tip just isn't strong enough to cope with the strain you're putting it under. Not only will it be impossible to accurately cast the feeder, but it's only a matter of time until the tip explodes into a thousand pieces!

To go feeder fishing properly you've got to use the right

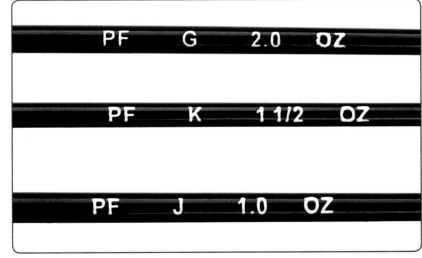

PF	G	2.0	OZ
PF	K	1 1/2	OZ
PF	J	1.0	OZ

quivertip for the stress you're putting it under. But your choice of quivertip also needs to be governed by a couple of other factors, namely the size of fish you're angling for and therefore the breaking strain of the line and the strength of the hooks you're using.

For example, if you're fishing a pond populated by lots of small fish and can therefore opt for light lines and small hooks, you need to use a light quivertip in conjunction with them. A heavy tip could easily place too much pressure on the line while playing a fish and cause it to snap.

At the other end of the scale, if you're fishing a powerful flowing river or a lake that's home to lots of large carp you'll need to step up your line and hook strength to cope with the situation. In this case a very fine tip will lack the inherent stiffness to hook and land a fish; it'll just bend until it can bend no more and may well break.

In fishing terms matching the strength of the line and hook to the rod/pole you're using is called balancing your tackle, and must be applied to every style of fishing discussed in this book. Your tackle should always be balanced to the size of fish you're catching and the stress you're loading on to your kit.

Think of it this way. You wouldn't make a cup of coffee with a garden spade – you'd almost certainly smash the mug while stirring in the sugar! It's exactly the same with fishing tackle. Don't use strong-arm kit for catching tiddlers and certainly don't use lightweight tackle for doing battle with monster fish.

Quivertips are usually made from one of two materials, carbon or glassfibre (shown above). In general the carbon tips are black and are a little stiffer and more brittle than the white glassfibre tips, which tend to be much softer.

In both cases the test curve (the weight it takes to bend the tip through 90°) is marked on the side of the tip. The higher the number, the heavier and stiffer the tip is – a 5oz tip is much stronger and stiffer than a 1oz tip, for example.

The guide below provides our recommendations for marrying different quivertips with the right size of feeder and strength of tackle.

Essential tackle

So that's the feeder rod and quivertip dealt with. Now we'll look at the other essential items of feeder fishing gear that you need. Over the page we look at specialist bits of tackle that are specific to feeder fishing.

Quivertip Rating	Species	Line	Feeder Weight	Hooks	Where to use
0.25oz ultra light	Roach, gudgeon and very small skimmer bream	Mainline 3lb, hooklink 1lb to 1.5lb	0.25oz to 1oz	Size 18 to 22 fine wire	Ponds and small canals
0.75oz light	Roach and larger skimmer bream	Mainline 3lb, hooklink 1.5lb	1oz to 1.5oz	Size 18 to 20 fine to medium wire	Small lakes
1oz medium light	Bream, small tench and small carp	Mainline 3lb to 4lb, hooklink 1.5lb to 2lb	1.5oz	Size 16 to 20 medium wire	Lakes
1.5oz to 2oz medium	Carp, tench and bream	Mainline 4lb, hooklink up to 3.5lb	1.5oz to 2oz	Size 14 to 18 medium wire	Lakes and slow rivers
2.5oz to 3oz medium heavy	Carp, bream, tench and chub	Mainline up to 6lb, hooklink 4lb to 5lb	Up to 3oz	Size 14 to 18 medium to heavy wire	Lakes and medium-size rivers
4oz heavy	Carp, chub and barbel	Mainline up to 8lb, hooklink 8lb maximum	3.5oz	Size 12 to 16 heavy wire	Lakes and big rivers
5oz to 7oz extra heavy	Big carp and barbel	Mainline 10lb plus, hooklink 10lb	4oz to 6oz	Size 8 to 12 heavy wire	Powerful rivers

Kit extras that'll get you geared up

In the float fishing chapter we've already looked at fixed spool reels and how to fill them with line, and what held true for that type of fishing is equally true for feeder fishing – with a few minor amendments.

Once again, a good quality fixed spool reel is essential, as feeder fishing places considerable strain on your tackle. It

should be fitted with a deep spool that holds plenty of line and is loaded with slightly heavier breaking strains, usually in the 4lb to 6lb range. As was outlined on the quivertip guide on the previous page, line of this breaking strain will cover the majority of fishing situations that you'll face. Once again the line you fill the reel with needs to sink, so speak to the tackle dealer to get the right product for the job.

Next you need to pick the feeder itself, and although there are lots of different designs we've simplified the choice down to the five main types that will cover most fishing situations.

1 The open-end feeder

The classic open-end feeder is a hollow plastic tube drilled with small holes. It's designed to be stuffed with a crumb groundbait and cast into the water, which quickly washes out the feed to attract fish to the hookbait.

In recent years a popular variant of the open-ender has been the cage feeder. Made from a plastic or metal mesh, this is designed for fishing in shallow waters or when a rapid release of bait is required, as its open construction allows the water to penetrate the feeder better and wash the bait out quickly.

2 The block-end feeder

Designed to carry live baits like maggots, and therefore commonly called the maggot feeder, this design features one or two caps that seal off both ends of the feeder. The plastic body is drilled with a number of holes that allow water to wash into it once it's cast out and give the maggots contained inside an escape route. Within seconds of landing on the bottom of the lake or river the maggots will be crawling out through the holes to lace the surrounding area with free offerings.

Compared to how far lightweight maggots can be accurately fired by catapult the much heavier block-end feeder allows you to place these tiny baits in a very small area at much greater range.

3 The flat feeder

This is a modern style of swimfeeder developed by top angler Andy Findlay and it has arguably established itself as the most effective type of feeder for stillwater fishing where carp, bream and tench are the dominant species.

Unlike traditional designs of open-end and block-end swimfeeders where the bait is stuffed inside the feeder, with the flat feeder the groundbait is packed on to a number of ribs that run on the outside of the frame. A metal base not

only ensures that the feeder can be cast a long way but also guarantees that it lands on the bottom of the lake the same way every time – the heavy base will be lying flat on the bottom of the lake, meaning that the groundbait plastered on to the upper surface will be open to attack by the fish.

It's an active style of feeder fishing that's most productive when you re-cast every minute or two to land a fresh payload of bait in the area you're fishing and thereby increase the feeding activity.

4 The Method feeder

This triangular-shaped feeder was a forerunner to the flat feeder inasmuch as the bait is stuck to the outside of the frame rather than being stuffed inside it.

Depending on the texture of groundbait packed around it this type of feeder can be used in a variety of stillwater fishing scenarios. For example, if a lightweight groundbait mix is used

that will collapse quickly once cast into the water, the method feeder can be used as a rapid fish catcher that's re-cast every couple of minutes to inject fresh bait into the water.

By contrast if a stickier groundbait mix is used which firmly grips the fins of the feeder you can afford to leave the feeder lying in the water for a long time. This tactic has proved very popular with anglers trying to tempt specimen-sized carp, tench and bream, as they can be confident that bait remains wrapped around the feeder long enough for the smaller population of big fish to find it.

5 The pellet feeder

This is the most recent adaptation of the swimfeeder and is something of a halfway house between the open-end

and block-end types, being capped at one end and open at the other.

This design of feeder is stuffed with specially softened mini pellets before being cast into the lake. Water then rushes into the frame of the feeder and washes out a neat pile of pellets to sit alongside the hookbait. This has proved to be a brilliant tactic for catching big bags of carp, bream and tench in still waters.

Rigging up ...

You now know what the main principle of feeder fishing is, the key items of kit you need, and what the main types of feeder are. Over the next 24 pages we'll detail various different feeder rigs that'll cover most of the fishing situations you'll be faced by.

The open-end feeder explained

Use strong 5–6lb mainline for repeated casting of an open-end swimfeeder.

For large bream, tench and carp a 5–6lb hooklink is required with a strong size 16–12 hook, the bigger the bait the bigger the hook. A two foot long hooklink is a good starting point. Lengthen or shorten it if you're not catching.

This is traditionally the most popular type of swimfeeder and it's not hard to see why. It's easy to set up and fill with attractive groundbait that most freshwater fish species are drawn to, it can be used in all still waters and it can be cast a long way.

The sequence below shows eight simple steps to produce a basic but very efficient running feeder rig and how to plug it with the groundbait that will attract fish to your hookbait. Over the page we look at groundbait in more detail, explaining what these feeds are and how to use them.

1 Thread the reel line through the feeder rod in the same fashion as described in Chapter 2 for the waggler float, then slide the line through the swivel on the top of the swimfeeder.

2 Thread the line through the top section of a Korum Quick Change Bead. This is a clever gadget that allows the hooklink to be attached and locked securely to the mainline very quickly. It's a two-piece bead in which the mainline is tied to one end while the other end sports a special hook that the hooklink is looped over; a small round bead then slides over the hook to trap the hooklink in place. To change or replace the hooklink you simply pull the two sections apart.

3 Tie on the bottom peg of the Quick Change Bead and attach a hook-to-nylon.

4 Slide the top part of the bead over the bottom section to trap the hooklink in place.

5 The finished set-up with the feeder resting against the Quick Change Bead.

6 Bait the hook – bury the feeder in groundbait and fill the frame with attractive crumb and loosefeed such as casters and chopped worms.

7 Pinch a layer of groundbait into each end of the feeder to make it stick firmly inside the feeder so that it won't fly out on the cast.

8 This is the baited rig ready for casting. It takes a few minutes to tie and start using.

Making groundbait

One of the key ingredients for many swimfeeder set-ups is groundbait. Stuffed inside or packed on the outside of the feeder frame, this highly attractive crumb collapses once it's cast into the water, sending out a potent plume of attractive flavours and smells that will draw fish to the area near the hookbait.

A few years ago the staple groundbait for most anglers was brown bread crumb. Once mixed with water it could be turned into a stodgy stuffing that could be packed inside a feeder along with a few samples of bait such as casters and hemp. However, although fish were attracted to the smell of the bread it wasn't hugely productive and was mainly used as a carrier for the morsels of food you added to it.

Times have changed. Walk into any tackle shop these days and you'll find shelves creaking under the weight of ready-mixed groundbait recipes that are made of much more complicated ingredients than plain brown bread crumb. Anglers have realised that the groundbait itself can be the main attractor, and not just a carrier for bits of food that might be added to the mix. Most modern groundbaits contain a potent variety of crushed sweet biscuits, fishmeal and a host of powdered flavours.

But it's not just the smell and flavour of the dry powder mix that sets different groundbaits apart. Depending on the particular blend of ingredients some groundbaits will also be stickier than others. This directly affects how the various groundbaits perform in the water. While some are designed to rapidly break down and throw out a short but very intense burst of aromas and flavours, other mixes cling to a feeder far longer in order to provide a more lasting source of attraction.

Over the next few pages we'll cover popular groundbait mixes that represent just some of the huge variety available. Suggestions are also given regarding the best way to use each of them for feeder fishing.

Fast-breakdown fishmeal

1 Tip the dry groundbait mix into a *round* bowl (because it has got no corners it's easier to mix the bait thoroughly this way). Make this your first job when you get to the swim you're going to fish.

2 Slowly add water, a little at a time, mixing the fishmeal with your hand as you do so. It's vital you don't over-wet this mix or it will stiffen into a very firm feed.

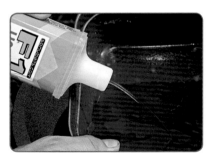

3 To boost the bait you can spruce up the mixing water by adding a dash of bait flavouring.

4 You're looking to create a moist – not *wet* – crumb, so make sure that the moisture is well mixed in.

5 The bait should be just about damp enough to hold together when squeezed...

6 ...But should break apart again if you give it a slight rub.

7 Loosefeed like casters can be added. Don't add maggots, as their movement stops the bait binding properly.

8 Micro pellets can also be added – use 2–3mm halibut pellets.

9 The bait is packed tightly inside a swimfeeder.

10 This type of mix will disintegrate very quickly in the water, emitting a highly attractive plume of smell. However, this will soon dissipate so you'll need to re-cast every minute or two. It's ideal for both the standard open-end feeder rig (page 70) and the flat feeder (page 76).

11 Big bream like this love groundbait, especially those that have a lot of fishmeal in them.

The block-end feeder explained

There are a number of different shapes and designs of block-end feeders, and the rig shown on pages 70/71 can be used with many models – just attach one of these feeders to the clip rather than an open-end feeder.

However, in recent years a new style of block-end feeder has been launched that's worthy of special attention in this manual – the inline bolt feeder from Drennan, which is a great fish catcher. As the sequence of pictures shows, it's an easy rig to tie but it is supremely efficient. By running the line straight through the swimfeeder then attaching a short hooklink baited with maggots, you soon have a hookbait surrounded by loosefeed as the grubs exit the feeder.

When a fish picks up the hookbait it pulls the line tight to the heavy feeder (it has a metal base) and hooks itself. The bite you get on the quivertip is an unmissable wrench round as the hooked fish reacts to the resistance by rushing away.

Here's how you put this rig together.

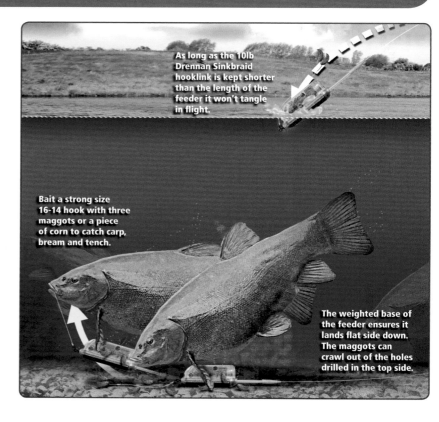

As long as the 10lb Drennan Sinkbraid hooklink is kept shorter than the length of the feeder it won't tangle in flight.

Bait a strong size 16-14 hook with three maggots or a piece of corn to catch carp, bream and tench.

The weighted base of the feeder ensures it lands flat side down. The maggots can crawl out of the holes drilled in the top side.

1 The kit you need – a Drennan Bolt Block-end feeder, size 16 Drennan Carp method hooks, size 9 E-S-P Uni-Link swivel and 10lb Drennan Super Specialist braid.

2 Thread the feeder's tail rubber down the reel line, followed by the feeder. The line runs through the centre of the feeder. The metal plate ensures that the feeder lands base down at every cast.

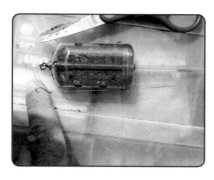

3 Cut off a length of braided line and use a grinner knot (see page 153) to tie on the hook. Hold the hook next to the end of the feeder and cut off the link so that it's fractionally shorter than the swimfeeder. This avoids tangles by stopping you tying a link longer than the feeder.

4 Tie the swivel on to the end of the hooklink with a Palomar knot (for details of which see pages 99–100). This simple knot is easy to tie with a short length of line.

5 Pull the swivel into the soft junction on the base of the feeder. This semi-fixes the hooklink to the feeder.

6 The finished rig. Note how the hooklink is around a centimetre shorter than the feeder. This reduces tangles on the cast.

7 Bait the hook with two or three red maggots and lift the cap off the feeder – the stem is flexible to make this easier. Grab a handful of maggots to load inside the feeder.

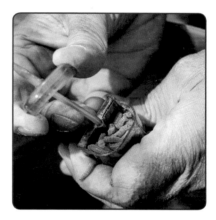

8 Fill the feeder but don't pack it tight with maggots. Leave a gap, as this helps the maggots wriggle better and exit the feeder quicker.

9 The baited rig ready to be cast. When a fish picks up the hookbait on such a short link, the line is pulled tight to the heavy feeder and the hook sinks home.

10 Tench are suckers for maggots. When they pick up the hookbait they pull the hooklink tight to the heavy swimfeeder and hook themselves. This is a very effective self-hooking rig.

The flatbed method feeder explained

In flight the rig won't tangle because the hooklink and bait are tucked inside the groundbait.

When they suck in the hair rigged bait they hook themselves against the feeder and bolt away – don't strike, just pick up the bending quivertip rod.

Fish like bream and carp dig into the groundbait coating.

Once again this is a simple rig to construct and follows the same principle as the inline bolt feeder shown on the previous spread.

The feeder is threaded on to the mainline before a swivel and a short hooklink is tied on the end. When the hookbait is picked up the fish hooks itself against the weight of the feeder and you get a rod-ripping bite.

However, one major difference with this rig is that the groundbait is packed on the outside of the feeder, and to make this job an awful lot easier a brilliant gadget called a Preston Innovations Quick-Release Method mould is used.

Here's what you do…

1 This is the basic rig – a Preston Innovations inline feeder threaded on the mainline with a swivel and short 3- to 5- inch hooklink of strong 6–9lb line tied to the end.

2 The swivel pulls into the end of the feeder to lock the rig together.

3 Lay a thin layer of fishmeal groundbait in the base of the mould.

4 Bait the hook and lay it and the hooklink on top of the feed. For a piece of meat like this use a size 12–16 hook.

5 Fill the mould with groundbait. Place the ribs of the feeder face down on the groundbait.

6 Press down on the metal base of the feeder to push it into the bait.

9 Here's the aerodynamically-shaped feeder rig ready to be cast.

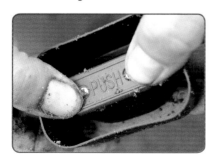

7 Turn the mould over and press the release button on the underside.

8 The feeder, now loaded with groundbait, is jettisoned.

Mixing the perfect flatbed feeder groundbait

The flatbed method feeder is a brilliant fish-catching tactic, but the groundbait packed on to it must be right for the job. Essentially the bait must be packed with attraction and must break down quite quickly to ensure that the hookbait is buried amid the feed to become available to feeding fish. Lots of groundbaits have been designed to do just this and most have a very fine fishmeal as their main ingredient.

This means that the groundbait must be mixed very carefully to create a groundbait with a soft texture that collapses quickly once underwater. Add a bit too much water and the bait can go too stiff and the breakdown can become very slow; add even more water and the bait can quickly become too sloppy to stick to the ribs of the swimfeeder.

However, get it right and the groundbait will stick to the feeder firmly but will still break down quickly once it's been cast out. This means that re-casting every couple of minutes is usually required with the flat feeder; only in winter, when fish aren't feeding so strongly, should you extend this to 10, 15 or even 20 minutes.

Be in no doubt – this is one of THE most productive tactics for catching carp and bream in well-stocked commercial fisheries.

1 Buy a purpose-made fine fishmeal groundbait such as Sonubaits Match Method Mix and tip the groundbait into a bowl.

2 Add water while vigorously mixing the two together.

3 Keep mixing until the feed stiffens into a moist, slightly sticky bait that forms a ball when squeezed.

4 Leave it to stand for 20 minutes to let the moisture soak through the bait.

5 You may need to add a bit more water if the feed dries out too much. However, you should add the water sparingly, to stop the bait getting too stiff.

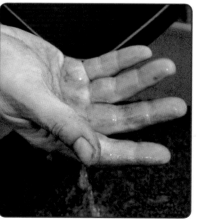

6 Get it right and fabulous carp like this will fall to the flatbed feeder.

The Method feeder explained

Use a short 3 to 5 inch long hooklink of strong 8lb-plus line and a heavy-duty size 10-14 hook. Mainline is 10–12lb to cast such a heavy feeder.

When a fish sucks up the hookbait on such a short link it hooks itself against the weight of the heavy Method feeder and it bolts away. Just pick up the rod and tighten into it.

This is the prop forward of the swimfeeder world – it's big, it's crude and it makes lots of noise!

The Method feeder was the forerunner to the flatbed

swimfeeder, and while it was originally designed to catch quite small carp it has now developed into a way of tempting specimen-sized carp, bream and tench. The way the tactic works is based around a stiff and sticky groundbait that's plastered to the triangular frame of an inline swimfeeder threaded on to heavy-duty 10lb-plus mainline. The idea is to cast out the loaded feeder and leave it for larger fish to locate. Sometimes this can take quite a while and it's not unusual to leave the feeder for 20 or 30 minutes between casts. On some waters this can even stretch to an hour or two.

It's bolted together in a similar fashion to the inline feeder rigs already detailed (pages 74/75) and it self-hooks fish that pick up the bait on the short hooklink and then pull against the weight of the feeder.

Overleaf we'll show you how to put the rig together and make the perfect Method feeder groundbait.

1 Here's the kit you need – Drennan Method feeders and strong, 3in ready-tied hooklinks made of 8lb-plus line and a size 10 to 14 hook.

2 Thread the feeder on to strong 10lb reel line. The line goes in the thin end of the feeder and comes out of the wide base.

3 Attach the short pre-tied hooklink to a size 8/10 swivel.

4 Tie the swivel on to the end of the mainline.

5 Pull the mainline to drag the swivel into the soft rubber base sleeve of the feeder.

6 Here's the finished rig. The feeder is threaded along the mainline with the short hooklink semi-fixed to the base of the feeder.

7 This Drennan model has two weighted vanes to ensure that it always lands on the deck. The hookbait is then laid next to the unweighted, plastic upper vane.

8 Push a baiting needle through an 8mm boilie hookbait and hook it on to a hair rig loop on the end of the hooklink (see Chapter 5 for full details of hair rigging).

9 Slide the boilie on to the hair rig and lock it in place with a plastic boilie stop slipped through the loop underneath the hookbait.

Making the perfect Method mix groundbait

To get the best from the Method feeder it's essential to use a groundbait that's firm and sticky. Not only is this texture needed in order to grip the feeder fins firmly enough to withstand casting a long way, it's also designed to ensure that the bait doesn't disintegrate the instant it hits the bottom of the lake. The idea is to give large fish enough time to find the feeder and dig out the hookbait, this tactic being responsible for the capture of some very big bream, tench and carp.

If your lake is a very prolific water packed with lots of 1–10lb carp or large shoals of smaller bream and tench, the flatbed method feeder is a better bet; but if your venue is home to a decent stock of large fish then the Method could well be your answer, especially in the warmer months when fish are feeding more positively.

Here's how you make a slow-breakdown specimen Method feeder mix:

1 Some groundbaits are labelled with the words 'Method Mix', which denotes that they form a much firmer mix if extra water is added. Speak to your tackle dealer to make sure you buy one that will mix into a firm feed.

2 Follow the same sequence of mixing the groundbait as is detailed for the fishmeal groundbait, except that you'll add more water to the Method mix.

3 Once again leave the mix to absorb the water, then add a bit more if needed. You want the mix to form a very firm ball when gripped in your hand. You may have to tweak the mix with more dry groundbait or water to get the right consistency.

4 Lay the baited feeder on a handful of groundbait, ensuring the plastic vane is pointing upwards with the two weighted vanes touching the groundbait.

5 Partially cover the frame of the feeder with groundbait, then fold the hooklink backwards and lay it on top of the feed.

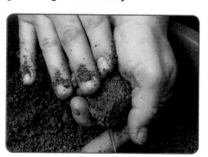

6 Pack more groundbait round the feeder, enclosing the hookbait in feed.

7 Shape the baited feeder to ensure that an aerodynamic ball of groundbait is created.

8 Cast out the loaded feeder and fish like this cracking 20lb carp can be yours.

The time-bomb river feeder explained

Use a 2–3ft long hooklink of 8lb-plus line with hair rigged pellets or boilies presented below a strong size 10–14 hook.

Strong mainline of at least 10lb is used to cast a heavy feeder and cope with snaggy rivers. The flow pushes out the groundbait.

A twist on the open-end feeder, the time-bomb feeder was developed for catching barbel in large rivers and has accounted for an incredible number of catches in recent years. It's included in this manual because it's such a beefed-up version of the open-ender that it deserves special consideration.

1 Keep the rig simple – just thread a large feeder on the reel line and leave it sliding above a large buffer bead and a swivel holding a 2–3ft long hooklink of 8lb line.

2 Here's the ingredients you need – a fishmeal/crushed pellet groundbait such as halibut pellet crush, some 4–6mm halibut pellets, hemp, and maybe a bit of halibut oil flavouring.

3 Pour the halibut crush into a mixing bowl.

4 Mix in water, a little at a time, until it starts to bind.

5 Add a handful of hemp and halibut pellets.

6 Blend the hemp and pellets into the fishmeal groundbait.

7 Stuff a large cage feeder with the fishmeal and pellet combo.

8 An alternative method is to cap a feeder with a thin layer of solid fishmeal groundbait.

9 Drop hemp, pellets and/or broken boilies into the feeder to sit on top of the groundbait layer.

10 Then cap the bait sandwich with another layer of groundbait.

Hookbaits for the time-bomb

Barbel love fishmeal groundbaits and hookbaits made from this potent ingredient. Be they boilies or pellets, the hookbaits shown here will all tempt barbel when used alongside fishmeal groundbait loaded with bits of similar loose offerings.

Be sure to try different variations of hookbait, as sometimes just a quick change of bait can make a huge difference.

1 There's no need to carry kilos of different hookbaits – a tub carrying fishmeal boilies and drilled 10–14mm pellets will suffice.

2 Hair-rigged boilies can also be great baits. Barbel especially love fishmeal and savoury baits – don't pick huge boilies, 10–14mm baits are ample.

3 If barbel on your water have been fished for a while with large pellets, try this advanced tip – place dabs of superglue on a couple of 6mm or 8mm halibut pellets.

4 Sandwich the hair rig loop between the two blobs of glue and carefully push the baits together. Don't get the glue on your fingers!

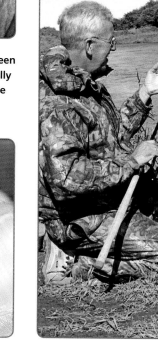

5 Repeat with two more pellets and you've got a small hookbait that mimics the baits you sandwich inside the feeder with groundbait.

6 On large rivers like this one, Yorkshire's River Wharfe, the fishmeal and pellet time-bomb is a productive barbel catcher.

The pellet feeder explained

Pellets have become the dominant bait on most still waters in the last few years and this feeder has been developed to take advantage of this. Whether you're fishing for carp, tench or bream pellets take some beating, as the fishmeal and oil they contain has an almost magnetic appeal to many coarse fish species.

The way this feeder works is that small feed pellets, usually 1mm or 2mm, are soaked in water for the same number of minutes as their diameter, for example 2mm micros should be soaked for two minutes before the water is drained away. Left to stand for at least 20 minutes (overnight is better still), the water slowly seeps through the pellet and turns the hard, dry bait soft and slightly sticky – this is the perfect texture for stuffing into the feeder and casting out. Once cast out water rushes into the tiny gaps between the soft pellets and washes them out of the feeder to lie alongside the hookbait. It's a great way to attract fish to the area.

This type of feeder offers the angler a great advantage over any other way of fishing with micro pellets, as you can cast a payload of bait way beyond the maximum distance you can catapult them. Like the other feeders we've described, the pinpoint placement of feed right next to the hookbait is unbeatable, and the pellet feeder has quickly established itself as one of the very best ways to catch carp in still waters.

It works best in the warmer months when fish are feeding particularly strongly, in which case regular and accurate re-casting every few minutes is essential to build up bait in the area and draw in more fish.

In colder months be more cautious – as you should be with all the feeder techniques outlined in this chapter. Reduce the frequency of casting to avoid overfeeding fish that are not likely to be ravenous in cold conditions. You might have to wait 10, 20 or even 30 minutes for a bite.

Here's how the rig is put together using one of the leading pellet feeders made by GURU.

Attaching the feeder to your mainline

As the sequence below shows, as long as you can tie a loop in your line you can complete the first part of the rig in a matter of seconds. These pictures show how to tie an elasticated feeder to the reel line.

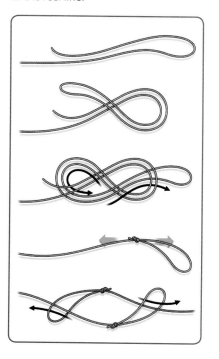

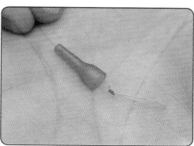

1 Follow this diagram to tie a figure-of-eight loop knot in the end of your mainline. Because the feeder is quite heavy and catches big fish you need to use 6lb mainline.

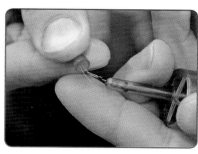

2 Thread a Guru tail rubber over the loop and slide it down the reel line. Place the loop over the metal wire clip on the top of the feeder stem.

3 Push the tail rubber on to the clip to trap the line in place. And that's it – job done!

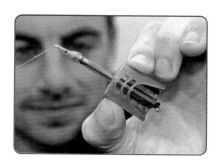

4 Here's the completed feeder, attached to the reel line ready to have the hooklink added. How easy is that?

Tying and attaching the hooklink

One of the most vital components of the pellet feeder is a short, 4in hooklink. As you'll see in the next sequence, this short trace is what presents the hookbait effectively and helps the rig to be such an efficient self-hooking tactic.

Here's how you tie the hooklink and attach it to the swimfeeder:

1 This is the equipment you need: GURU QM1 size 12 hooks, scissors, micro bait bands, GURU micro silicone tubing (0.3mm diameter) and Shimano Antares Silk Shock line (0.2mm diameter, breaking strain 9.4lb).

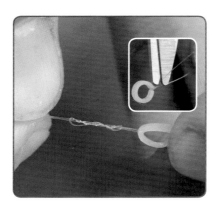

2 Tie the band on the end of the hooklink line – use a four-turn grinner knot (see page 153 for a grinner knot), as it ensures the band sits straight on the hair. Pull the knot tight and trim off the line (inset picture).

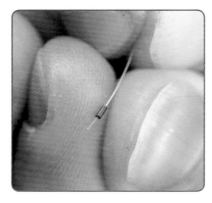

3 Cut off 10–12in (25–30cm) of line and thread a 3–5mm piece of micro tubing on to the hooklink line.

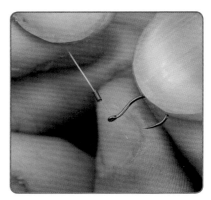

4 Thread the hooklink through the back of the hook eye.

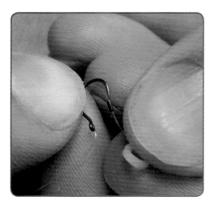

5 To trap the tubing and line to the hook push the hook point through the opening in the tubing.

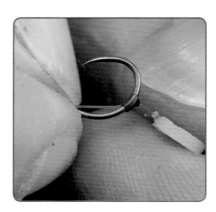

6 Slide the silicone tube round to the bottom of the shank. Note the circular shape of the QM1 hook, which ensures a solid hook-hold.

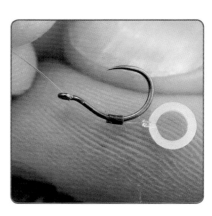

7 The bait band should be positioned just below the bend of the hook.

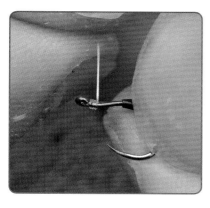
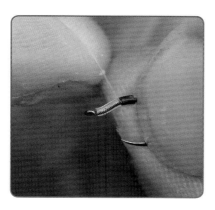
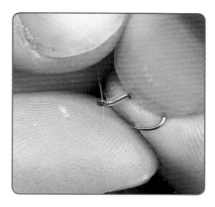

8 Whip the hooklink line down the shank 10 to 12 times, making sure the first turn goes down the side of the hook eye opposite the gap where the wire is bent to form the eye.

9 Pinch the coils of line and thread the end of the hooklink line back through the rear of the hook eye. Moisten and pull tight.

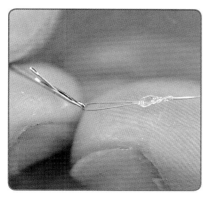
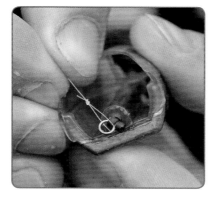

10 Tie a figure-of-eight loop knot (see diagram on page 87) in the end of the hooklink.

11 Put the hooklink loop over the metal ring on the end of the elasticated section running through the centre stem of the pellet feeder.

12 With the loop trapped below it, thread the hook, hair rig and bait band through the ring.

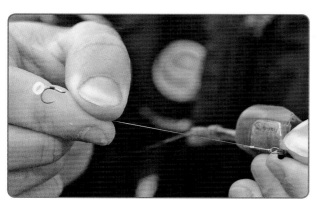

13 Moisten the line and slowly pull the hooklink tight to the ring.

14 Here's the finished rig ready to be stuffed with bait and cast out. Note the 4in hooklink hanging below the feeder.

Baiting a pellet feeder

At the heart of the pellet feeder's success is the bait itself – pellets, of course.

The swimfeeder is designed to carry a payload of softened carp feed pellets. Once loaded inside the weighted feeder these small baits can be cast way beyond normal catapulting range, and this has proven itself to be a fabulously effective technique, especially when cast tight to distant islands.

To make the feeder work you have to soften the feed pellets first to render them slightly sticky before you pack them carefully into the feeder. Here's how you do it…

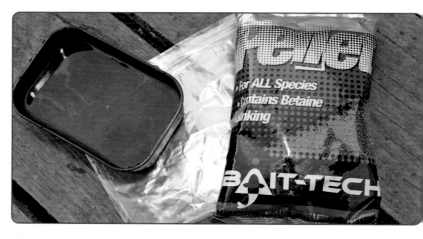

1 To create perfect soft pellets all you need is an 800g bag of 2mm micro pellets, half a pint of water and a plastic bag or sealable container.

2 Start the softening process by tipping the pellets into the bag.

3 Then pour the water into the bag.

4 Shake the pellets and water for a couple of minutes, leave them to stand for a few minutes, and then shake them again. This distributes moisture over all the pellets.

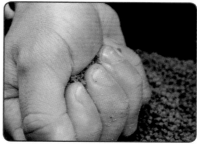

5 Leave the pellets to soften for at least 25 minutes, or better still prepare them the night before fishing. The pellets will soften and will stick loosely together if squeezed.

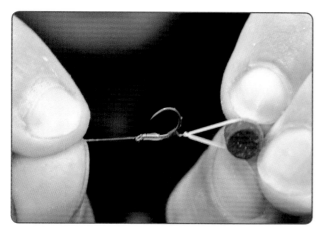

6 Place a 6mm Bait-Tech halibut pellet in the bait band on the end of the hooklink.

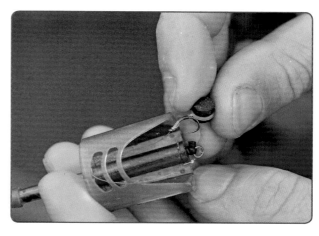

7 Tuck the hooklink inside the feeder but keep the hook and bait hanging outside.

8 Lay the base of the feeder on the softened pellets, scoop the baits inside, and gently push the pellets so that they grip the feeder and trap the hooklink inside.

9 Lay the hookbait and hook on the first layer of pellets.

10 Cover the hookbait with a second layer of pellets and give the bait a slight squeeze to stick the baits together.

11 Here's the finished rig ready for casting. Note how the entire hooklink is trapped within the feeder and the pellets are contained within the frame. This is vital when casting tight to islands or margins when the loaded feeder might hit or brush vegetation as it hits the water; with no hanging hooklink, and the bait enveloped inside the plastic feeder, the bait won't get knocked out of the feeder and the hook won't snag up.

Casting accurately with a pellet feeder

The pellet feeder possesses three main advantages.

Firstly, it delivers a small quantity of food in a very tight area – this focuses fish's attention on the hookbait.

Secondly, the GURU pellet feeder has a specially weighted base that ensures it flies like a dart with great accuracy.

Thirdly, and most importantly, the frame of the feeder encloses all the feed in a plastic shell and allows the hookbait to be secured inside the feeder too. This is hugely beneficial when casting tight to islands or marginal vegetation when it's easy to accidentally hit or brush reed stems, grass and branches that are lying in the water. Not only is it far more likely that the bait will remain trapped inside the feeder (it would get knocked off the outside of a Method feeder) and still be fishable, but it also reduces the chances of the rig getting stuck on the snag or island.

To get the most out of this fabulous tactic it's essential you can cast accurately to land the feeder tight to the island or a distant margin of the fishery.

The sequence below shows how you can guarantee casting accuracy using a leger weight, the clip on the reel spool and a piece of line. This system can also be used to ensure casting accuracy with other types of swimfeeder or leger weight.

1 Before you start fishing tie a 0.5–1oz leger weight on the end of your reel line.

2 Cast at the feature you want to target but 'brake' the flow of line to ensure it lands short by a few yards.

3 Pull a few feet of line off the reel and slide it into the clip on the side of the spool.

4 Re-cast at the feature and hold your rod straight up in the air. As the line pulls tight to the clip the flight of the leger is halted; lower your rod to let it hit the water a little nearer the feature. Repeat step 3 and re-cast, inching your way towards the feature a few feet at a time until the leger lands where you want the feeder to go. Replace the leger with the pellet feeder rig and you're in business!

5 Remember to tie a piece of monofilament line as a marker on the mainline where it's clipped up. If you hook a big fish and have to unclip to give it line, it's a simple job to re-clip the reel line where the marker is positioned.

1 The feeder flies through the air like a bullet, and the hooklink can't tangle as it's enclosed in the soft pellets.

2 Splashing down, the feeder can brush the vegetation without getting snagged up on it.

3 On the bottom the pellets tumble out and give the fish a neat pile of pellets to home in on.

Now that you've seen how to tie a pellet feeder rig, load the feeder with soft pellets and accurately cast it every time. This diagram shows you what happens beneath the water.

Enclosing the hookbait inside the feeder helps to avoid tangles on the cast and makes it easier to cast very close to islands or reed beds where the feeder might brush overhanging vegetation as it enters the water.

Once on the deck the water soaks into the softened pellets and causes them to swell – the baits will then tumble out of the feeder along with the hookbait.

In this way a highly tempting pile of pellets is created as a focus for the fish's feeding behaviour; as the carp suck in the loosefeed they take the hookbait at the same time.

As soon as they straighten the short hooklink and pull the line tight to the feeder the weight in the frame pulls the hook home – a blistering bite will be the result!

How to cast a feeder

You've now got six different feeder rigs in your fishing armoury – you probably won't need another one for the rest of your angling career!

However, it's important that you know how to cast a swimfeeder accurately every time. We've already looked at this subject briefly on page 92, but here we take an in-depth look at casting technique with top match angler Steve Ringer.

1 Before you attach your feeder, clip a leger weight (right) on to the mainline to find your casting range as shown on the previous page. This avoids scattering bait all over your swim.

2 With the line clipped up and the feeder re-attached, line up the rod with a far bank marker that won't move, such as a swim platform, tree, reed bed or island.

3 Gain some momentum on the leger weight by swinging it in front of you with a 3ft drop from rod tip to leger.

6 The rod tip acts as a brake as the line pulls into the clip, cushions it, and allows you to drop the feeder on a tight line close to the feature you aimed at. You can then wind six turns of line directly on to the reel to act as a buffer to be released if you hook a big fish.

4 Swing the feeder straight behind you and punch the rod at the marker, releasing the line from the open spool as the rod reaches the 45° angle.

5 Watch the leger weight flying through the air and just before it hits the water pull the rod back smartly to point the rod directly up in the air.

7 Casting accurately with a swimfeeder helps Steve catch great fish like this mirror carp. You could land them too!

Setting up your seat box or chair

When you're fishing with a quivertip rod you need to set yourself up on the bank so that you can see and react to a bite.

The first stage of this involves arming yourself with an adjustable metal bankstick that has a ridged rod rest screwed into it. This might seem like a relatively small and unimportant piece of kit but it's vital to good feeder fishing. When you've cast out a swimfeeder and you're waiting for a bite you need to place the rod on a platform that holds its tip rock solid so that the merest twitch on the tip will be obvious to you – this is where a solid rod rest comes into play.

The sequence below shows how to use a rod rest correctly when feeder fishing. It's a vital piece of tackle that's frequently misused, but the very best anglers take a great deal of care about positioning their rest in exactly the right place.

1 Screw a ridged rod rest into a thick metal bankstick. Push it firmly into the ground at a slight angle to your seat box or chair and the spot you will aim the feeder at.

2 When you cast out and the line pulls tight to the clip on the side of the spool it's a simple job to lower the rod in an almost straight line and drop it on the rod rest. To see a bite you only need to put a gentle curve in the quivertip, so it only needs to be at a slight angle to the location of the feeder.

Five advanced tips for quivertip success

1 THE WRONG ANGLE

Many anglers place their rod on a rest parallel to the water, but there are three clear problems with doing this.

Firstly, to put the rod on the rest you have to move it a long way from its final casting position straight in front of your face. This makes it easy to accidentally move the feeder while you're doing this, thereby pulling your hookbait away from the feed.

Secondly, while you concentrate on the quivertip in this position you can't easily glance at the spot you've cast to because you're facing in the opposite direction. This makes it harder for you to gauge fish activity in the spot you're targeting. By contrast, having the tip almost pointing at the area you've cast to means that you can occasionally glance straight up to scan the water for signs of fish life in the area where the feeder is.

Finally, when a rod is positioned along the margins of the lake the space left for a sweeping strike is far more limited than it is for an angler pointing the rod forward.

2 TOO TIGHT

Here's another common mistake. Many anglers put far too much tension on the line and bend their quivertip right round – this has the effect of making the tip much stiffer, which not only makes it less responsive to a biting fish but may also put too much pressure on the line, which a shy-biting fish may feel. If they do they'll instantly reject the hookbait.

So slacken off a little – the tip should have a slight curve in it (above left), not a U-bend (above right)!

3 BEAT HARD BANKS

If your seat box or fishing chair has levelling legs fitted to it you can attach a quivertip arm. This can make it easier to fine-tune the position of the rod rest and also allows you to

create a rigid base for the rod if you're fishing on a hard bank that you can't push a bankstick into.

4 MOVEMENT CAN SPARK BITES

A heavy swimfeeder is designed to pin your hookbait to the bottom and produce a static bait presentation, which is what you want ... or is it?

When fish are reluctant to eat, twitching your feeder across the lake bed can spark a response as the slight movement of the feeder dislodges and disturbs the bait as well as spreading it out in a narrow strip of feed on the bottom. The hookbait will also be dragged into this channel of bait.

To twitch a feeder, pull on the mainline behind the front rod ring rather than by lifting the rod and pulling back on it (pictured top right); this gives you maximum control on how far you move the feeder, as you only want to nudge it along the bottom a few inches. By contrast, if you pull back on the rod this results in a build-up of tension as the rod bends and the swimfeeder remains unmoved. This tension will eventually reach a critical pressure point, and the feeder will tend to jump rather than twitch along the bottom. This can cause the line to tangle and is likely to pull the whole rig,

including your hookbait, away from the feed that's fallen out of the feeder. A rig that suddenly leaps off the bottom is also likely to spook any fish in the area.

Twitching the bait by teasing back the line is also made easier if you have the rod pointing at a slight angle to the water rather than running parallel with it, as the bending tip won't absorb the pressure you put on the line and you'll focus more controlled pressure on the feeder itself.

5 SIT ON YOUR HANDS

One of the most naturally gifted coarse anglers to have ever walked the planet was a man called Ivan Marks. If ever there was a person who could 'think like a fish' it was Ivan.

When he was fishing for large species, especially bream and carp, one of Ivan's greatest nuggets of advice was to 'sit on your hands and wait for a proper bite'. This tip was born from an understanding that when big fish moved into a baited area it was inevitable they'd bump into the line cutting through the water and running down to the swimfeeder. Often called 'line bites', these collisions produce twitches, taps and pulls on the quivertip that can easily be mistaken for a true bite. Of course, an angler striking at these false indications will fail to hook anything, as the fish isn't holding the hookbait in its mouth.

Instead Ivan urged anglers to read the indications on the tip and wait for a positive pull round to indicate that a fish had grabbed hold of the bait and was moving off with it – his advice to 'sit on your hands' urged anglers to ignore line bites.

It takes restraint not to react to the moving quivertip, but over time you'll learn to distinguish what line bites look like and you'll only strike when a fish actually picks up your bait.

Sit on your hands or fold your arms as you wait for a bite.

Legering

A very similar style of angling to swimfeeder fishing is known as legering. The same rods, reels and end tackle can be used for legering, and in fact the only real difference is that instead of attaching a feeder to line you use a bunch of large split shot or a heavy lead weight known as a leger.

The two picture sequences below show how to use a straight leger in a lake and how to tie up a link leger for use in rivers.

The straight leger

This is a set-up used by many anglers in midwinter when fishing on commercial day-ticket still waters traditionally gets harder.

When it's cold fish will move around a lot less and will therefore need to eat less food to refuel. In this situation casting out a swimfeeder packed with bait can provide the fish with too much food, as they fill up on the bait spilling out of the feeder long before they take the hookbait. This is when a legered bait can be worthwhile.

With a heavy leger attached to the line to provide casting weight, you cast out your bait with a quivertip rod and tighten up to the leger lying static on the bottom. If a fish picks up the hookbait it pulls the line, tugs on the fine quivertip and you get a bite – just as you would with a swimfeeder.

Use a visual hookbait with the straight leger, such as sweetcorn presented on a Quickstop hair rig (see page 100). If a carp or bream sees this shiny bait they'll often pick up a single morsel.

Here's how you set up a simple straight leger…

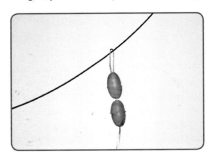

1 Slide two rubber float stops off the wire loop they're supplied on and on to your 4–5lb mainline.

2 Thread a 0.5oz to 1oz leger weight on to the line behind the leger stops.

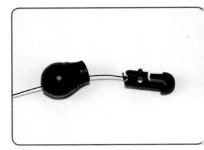

3 Slip the top part of a Korum Quick Change Bead on the line and tie on the lower connector section.

4 Slip your hooklink loop on to the connector, push the bead together and you're in business!

5 The rig is baited and cast out. Some top anglers such as Andy Findlay catapult a few pieces of loosefeed corn around the leger to advertise the lone hookbait.

6 Carp like this will come to the straight leger in winter. It's a simple tactic but one that works well when it's very cold.

The link leger

Roaming small rivers for chub is one of the purest forms of fishing. It's just you, the fish, a wild landscape, the minimum of tackle and lots of walking – magic stuff.

Dai Gribble (left) is an expert in this roving style of fishing so we picked his brains to discover how he catches.

KEEP IT SIMPLE

One of the most appealing aspects of small river chubbing is that complicated rigs aren't needed. Here's a step-by-step guide to tying Dai's link leger…

1 You only need five items – 6lb Korum Reel Line, size 6 Korum S3 hooks, John Roberts Soft Leger Stops, Preston Innovations double SSG shot and SSG shot.

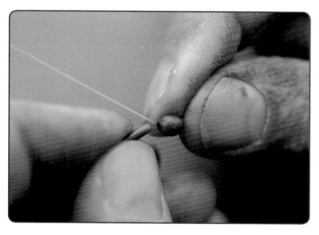

2 Start by sliding the John Roberts leger stop bead on the mainline.

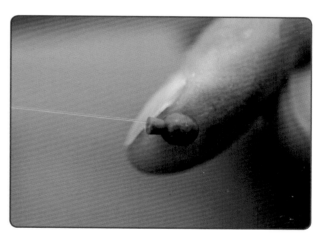

3 Lock it 2–3ft (60–90cm) up the line using the peg supplied.

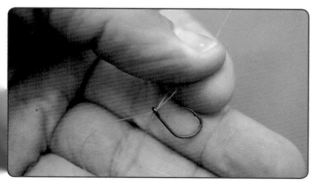

4 Double the reel line through the eye of the S3 hook – this is stage one of tying a Palomar knot.

5 Tie a simple overhand knot in the loop but don't pull it tight.

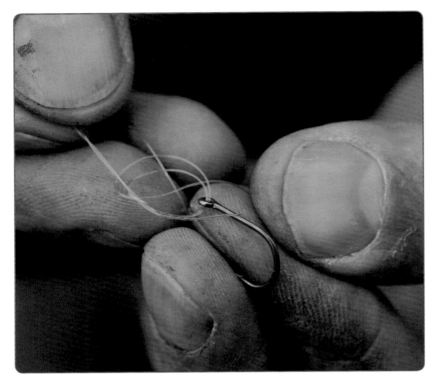

6 Take the tag loop and pull it over the hook bend and point.

7 Wet the knot and slowly pull it tight – you've just tied a Palomar knot.

8 Now cut off the 5–6in (12–15cm) tag of line, but don't throw it away.

9 Loop the tag over the mainline just above the leger stop.

10 Nip the required number of split shot on to the tag loop – two or three SSG shot is a good starting point on most rivers.

11 The finished rig is super-simple but very effective.

BREAD'S THE BAIT

In all but flood conditions, when the water is chocolate-coloured and he uses a bait with a lot more smell, a sliced white loaf is Dai's top hookbait. A fluffy chunk of flake wrapped around a size 6 hook masks the hook but is still soft enough to strike through. Here's how you hook it…

1 Tear off a square inch (about 5cm²) of thick-sliced flake.

2 Nip the flake firmly around the top of the shank. Fold the flake in half and lay the hook on it.

3 Leave the point exposed and the base fluffy.

BAITING UP

In most swims Dai relies on the hookbait to tempt a bite, but if fish need coaxing to feed he adds two walnut-sized nuggets of bread mash.

1 Put two slices of bread in your net and soak it.

2 Grip the soggy slices and squeeze out the excess water.

3 Now use your fingers to mash up the wet bread.

4 The consistency you want with the air expelled and different sized chunks of mash.

Hookbaits for feeders

There are dozens of different baits that can be used on a swimfeeder rig, and the natural baits shown in the float fishing section can also be very good with a feeder.

However, over the next four pages we give four suggestions that will help you catch lots of quality fish – especially if the fishery you visit holds larger species like carp, tench and barbel that like to eat bigger items of food.

Of particular interest to the improving angler is the fact that these ideas don't even feature a bait going directly on the hook itself. Instead it sits on a short piece of line hanging below the hook. Called a 'hair rig', this set-up was

invented in the early 1980s and changed coarse fishing forever, since it allowed anglers to use much bigger baits without masking any part of the hook. The resulting exposed hook point is far more efficient at hooking fish like carp, bream and barbel that feed by sucking up mouthfuls of mud and silt and then filtering out what's edible.

In recent years the basic hair rig (which was originally tied with a ladies' hair so that it was super fine and ensured the bait moved naturally!) has undergone many developments.

When dealing with the pellet feeder on page 88 we showed you how to tie a basic hair rig, but the variations below provide some alternative methods.

The Quickstop hair rig

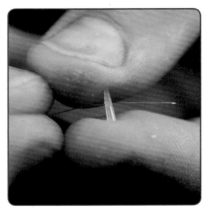

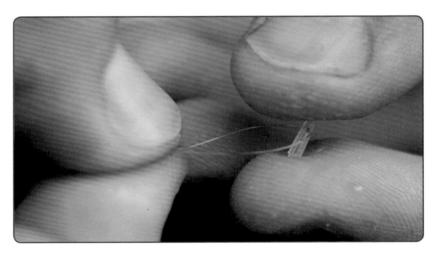

1 Thread the line through the hole in the Korum Quickstop bait bayonet.

2 Fold the line back on itself.

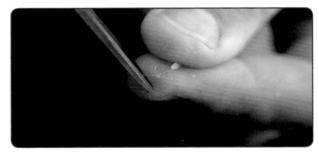

3 Form an overhand knot to lock the Quickstop in place.

4 Pull the knot tight to trap the bayonet in place at the end of the hooklink. Trim the tag end.

5 The Quickstop sits in a tiny loop on the end of the line.

6 Repeat the knotless knot procedure shown with the basic hair rig (pages 88/89) to leave the Quickstop hanging below the hook bend.

7 Use a metal bait punch to drill out a cylinder of luncheon meat.

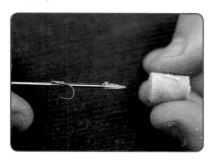

8 Push the special Quickstop needle into the hollow chamber inside the Quickstop.

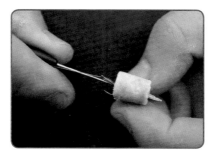

9 Drive the pointed end of the stop through the luncheon meat.

10 Rotate the Quickstop so that it lies flat to the bait.

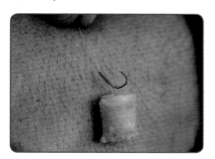

11 Slide the bait down the hair rig to sit on top of the flat platform.

12 Single pieces of sweetcorn can also be used...

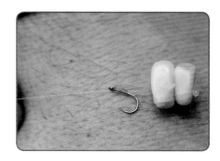

13 ...as can double pieces of corn or soft hooker pellets. This is a very secure hookbait best used for carp, tench or bream when feeder fishing or legering.

Ready-tied hooklinks for the feeder

Many different types of ready-tied hooklinks are available that already feature a hair rig and a special gadget to secure the bait for casting.

The picture sequence below demonstrates one of the best hookbait-mounting systems on the market, Middy's Las-Soo ready-made hooklink. This is a quick and easy way to mount a variety of baits which is especially good for feeder fishing, as it grips the bait firmly enough to withstand casting and hitting the water.

Here's how you use it…

Las-Soo your bait

1 Hard pellets can be used with the Las-Soo, but one of the best baits is a 6–8mm mini boilie. Score a shallow groove around the bait.

2 The Middy Las-Soo features a rubber stop sliding on the loop of line hanging below the hook. Put the mini boilie inside the loop with the line in the groove.

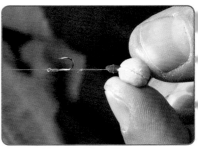

3 The stop is slipped down the line to trap the bait tightly in place. To change the bait push the rubber stop towards the hook to reopen the loop.

Get the best from your feeder fishing

You now have a comprehensive guide to the tackle you need, six rigs that'll do the job in just about any fishery, and a host of bait suggestions that have a proven catch record. But before wrapping up the chapter it's pertinent to offer a few words of advice that will help you combine all this information to ensure that you get the most out of this style of fishing.

If you remember these few pointers and always ensure they're part of your feeder fishing routine the technical lessons described here will be far more productive…

1 BE ACCURATE
Take your time when casting each loaded feeder to ensure that every payload of bait lands in a tight area. This concentrates feeding activity in one area and ensures you don't scatter bait all over the peg, which can pull fish away from your hookbait and reduce catches.

2 BE ACTIVE
Many anglers have a tendency to adopt a passive angling style when they use the feeder.

Because a feeder will carry quite a bit of bait and lie static on the bottom it's easy to settle in behind the rod and just wait for something to happen. This is a big mistake.

The best anglers adopt an almost metronomic regularity to their casting to keep refreshing the bait and to provide a visual stimulus to spark more feeding activity.

In late spring to early autumn, when water temperatures are warmer and fish usually feed strongly, casting every minute or two is usually recommended. In the winter months you can re-cast less frequently. As a general rule the colder the water gets the less the fish will feed and the

longer you can wait between casts. In this case casting every 10 to 20 minutes is likely to be a reliable option.

3 DON'T ALWAYS STRIKE
This gem of advice flies in the face of general fishing principles but it can be a vital skill.

In most cases the flat feeder, Method feeder and inline block-end feeder will produce dramatic bites where the fish wrench the quivertip right round. This is because the short hooklinks used with these rigs are semi-fixed to a heavy swimfeeder, and when fish pick up the bait they almost always hook themselves against the weight of the feeder and instantly bolt away.

If you react by striking in the traditional manner you compound the force being exerted against the line – fish are racing off one way, and you strike in the opposite direction. This can deliver far too much pressure for your tackle to withstand and you either snap the line or pull the hook out of the fish. Either way all you're left with is a story of the one that got away!

The solution to this is simple – DON'T STRIKE!

Because the fish is already hooked you don't need to strike the hook home – just pick up the rod and ease the tight line a bit tighter still to set the hook properly.

This can also be a good idea when fishing the time-bomb feeder in a river for barbel, as these fish tend to be very bold feeders and often tear off downstream with a bait in their mouth – don't strike, just pick up the rod, tighten the line and hang on for a wild ride!

POLE FISHING

Essential kit for pole fishing — 108

Elasticating — 112

Shotting up a pole rig — 118

Know your floats — 120

Making a pole rig — 122

Balancing your tackle — 126

Setting up for pole fishing — 128

Plumbing for pole fishing — 132

The importance of feeding — 134

Catching fish on the pole — 138

Essential kit for pole fishing

When mankind first caught a fish on a stick using some type of line with a hook tied on the end the first fishing pole had been invented. And although modern carbon poles are high-tech creations that use space-age technology they're still using essentially the same principles as with that first stick pole.

Unlike swimfeeder and float fishing which use a rod, reel and a castable line to launch the bait into the water, a pole is essentially a super-long 'stick' with the rig tied directly to the end.

Instead of the hookbait being cast – as it is with a float or feeder – a baited pole rig is placed where you want it. You simply reach the pole and baited rig out to the spot you want to fish and lower it into the water. Easy.

However, with no requirement to cast out the rig there's also no need to place a large float or feeder on the line so that you have enough weight to gain momentum for casting. Consequently a pole rig can be set up to be so sensitive that it gives you an alert the moment a fish touches your hookbait.

To continue the boxing analogy used in the previous chapter, while swimfeeder fishing is heavyweight when compared to a lightweight waggler float, a pole rig is a featherweight in comparison to the waggler.

Let's start our trip into pole fishing territory by looking at the tackle you need, starting with the pole itself…

Buying guide – what to look for in a pole

While modern poles adhere to the basic principle of the first 'stick pole', that's where any similarity ends. The technology that's been poured into carbon pole construction is at the forefront of the fishing industry.

In the last 20 years advances in carbon technology have been wide-ranging and rapid thanks to the huge amounts of money spent on research and development by the space, military, motor racing and aeroplane industries. This technology has trickled down to the fishing industry, where companies have used advances in carbon fibre to construct light and strong poles that no longer cost a fortune. Which means that there has never been a better time to buy one.

Whatever pole you buy the basic construction will be the same: a number of interlocking sections are supplied that allow the pole to be used at a variety of lengths. The more sections you put on, the further the pole reaches.

Apart from a few short, specialist margin poles that are solely designed to be used down the edges of lakes, most modern poles have a maximum length of 12m to 14m, but some will reach 16m or more. It's not unheard of for top anglers to fish at 18m or 19m! Compare that to a standard waggler float rod, which measures just 13ft (just over 4m).

When shopping for a pole you have to wade through a vast array of different products and your choice will be made all the more complicated by the trade-off that exists between what you pay and the quality and length of pole you get.

The common mistake made by many first-time pole buyers is that they simply look for the longest pole they can afford – they don't stop to ask if that pole is useable at that length, nor do they ask themselves if they actually need a pole that long.

It's a matter of scientific fact that the longer a pole gets and the more section joints it contains, the heavier it becomes, the more it will sag, and the more pull gravity will exert on it. So, for instance, it's much harder work to hold a 16m pole than a pole measuring 11m or 12m.

Although it's a broad generalisation that overlooks some of the finer details of pole technology, it's also true that the more expensive a pole is the better the quality of the carbon used in its construction. This means that the more you spend the lighter and more user-friendly a pole will be.

To help you make the right choice it's essential to test poles before you buy one, so you must visit a tackle dealer, sit on a seat box and hold a variety of manufacturers' poles at different lengths to get a feel for how comfortable you are when holding them.

Don't repeat the mistake of just buying the longest pole you can afford, and don't buy a pole which is longer than you need. It's almost a certainty that a 16m pole will not be as good at 12m as a pole of the same price that has a *maximum* length of 12m. It's also a waste of money to buy a 16m pole if you don't need a pole of that length or if it's too heavy for you to comfortably fish with. A far better bet would be to spend the same amount of money on a shorter pole of higher quality.

Finesse or power?

Apart from the length and price of a pole there's another key factor that should influence your decision – its strength.

Like float fishing rods, modern carbon poles can be roughly split into two camps: those made with power in mind for catching strong fish like carp and tench, and those that are much lighter and stiffer for catching smaller silverfish species like roach and bream. Commonly referred to respectively as 'power or carp poles' and 'silverfish or match poles', you need to think about the fishing you're planning to do and let the dealer know what you're most likely to be catching.

A carp pole will generally be made with sections that have thicker walls made from stronger grades of carbon cloth. This makes the pole strong, but it also adds to the weight and makes it less stiff.

A silverfish pole by contrast will have much thinner walls made from fewer wraps or a thinner grade of carbon cloth. It will be lighter than a carp pole, will sag less and will be stiffer.

A power carp pole will be the wisest choice for the majority of anglers, unless you only fish waters where small fish dominate or you can afford to buy a pole of each type. A carp pole is far more versatile and suitable for anglers fishing modern managed still waters.

While a carp pole can be used to catch small fish, a silverfish pole could be smashed to pieces by a big carp – replacement sections are too expensive to risk this!

And what about the extras?

Most pole manufacturers now sell the majority of their poles in packages that include a number of extras, and the value of these must be considered before you buy a pole. It's obviously preferable to buy a pole supplied with a selection of 'top kits' – these are the thin end sections that the rig is connected to, and having two or three kits allows you to set up different rigs and therefore have the ability to switch between them in seconds.

You should also look for top sections that have different ratings of strength. As a general rule you want more 'power kits' that are suitable for landing large carp or tench, but it's also useful to have a 'match kit' that's softer, thinner and more suitable for catching smaller species.

Finally, many pole packages are supplied with a 'cupping kit' (below), a really useful piece of equipment that should be seen as an essential part of any purchase. It's an extra end section of pole that's designed to have a deep cup screwed into it – bait is placed in this cup before it's shipped out to the area you want to fish and upended. This is a great way to loosefeed your swim quickly and with pinpoint accuracy. Ideally the cupping kit should also have an adjustable length so that it can be matched to the length of the top kits you fish with. This ensures your loosefeed and rig goes in exactly the same spot.

So which should you buy?

As we've already stressed in this manual, choosing a major item of tackle such as an expensive carbon pole is better done with the advice of a good tackle dealer. However, as a general guide the majority of anglers will find a 12.5m to 14.5m pole is long enough. It will ideally have at least three top kits (two power kits and one match kit), and it will be supplied with a purpose-made cupping kit.

As for how much you spend, some poles cost a fortune and are unnecessary for all but the best competition anglers who expect to recover the cost by winning lots of money in matches. At the other end of the price spectrum there are super-cheap packages that offer lots of pole for not a lot of money. However, while some can be great bargains others don't deliver meaningful quality and soon fail.

It's usually sound advice to buy a pole that's a little more expensive than the cheapest models, as that way you should also get somewhat better quality – a good tackle dealer should advise you honestly.

What else do you need?

1 A seat box with a footplate and leg-levelling system

Fishing chairs are useless for pole fishing – the backrest gets in the way when you slide the pole out or ship it back in again to land a fish or change the hookbait. A seat box is far better, especially if it has an adjustable leg system to enable you to level it up on uneven ground. A range of important accessories can also be attached to these legs and the footplate at the front is an essential platform for your feet.

On page 130 we'll describe how you hold a pole comfortably to avoid the blight of a painful back. The value of the footplate will then become obvious. And when, on pages 136/37, we show you how to loosefeed bait while holding the pole the value of the accessories that fit on to the legs will also become clear.

2 A twin-leg pole roller

When you ship your pole in or slide it back out again you need to run it over a stable pole roller that supports the

weight of the pole. The picture sequence on page 129 will explain just why a roller is so important for this job.

Large V-shaped rollers are available but a more stable choice is a wider roller braced by legs at either end.

3 A pole sock

Not something to keep your pole snuggly on a cold winter's

morning, but a cheap and really useful pocket that's fixed on the front of your seat box to hold the pole securely when you unship the end sections.

4 A pole pot

This tiny plastic pot is slipped on to the end section of your pole and holds a pinch of bait.

When the rig is shipped out to the spot you want to fish the pole is rotated to drop the contents of the pot into the water right next to the rig. They're a very cheap but utterly essential piece of kit. Don't go pole fishing without one!

5 An elastication kit

Each top kit of your pole will need to be fitted with a length of elastic running down the inside of the top two or three sections. This is one of the most important pieces of all pole tackle and over the page we'll show you how to elasticate a top kit.

Elasticating

When you hook a big fish on the pole there's really only one thing that gets in the way of you losing it – the elastic shock absorber running through the top kit of the pole.

Strong and stretchy, this elastic is designed to absorb the runs of a hooked fish to stop it breaking the line or pulling the hook out. With every move the fish makes the elastic goes with it, but the instant the fish runs out of steam the elastic contracts and pulls the fish back towards the pole. This saps the energy of a feisty fish, allowing a patient angler to play out and land some big fish on the pole.

As was explained earlier, pole choice is a difficult business, but one of the key things to look for is that you buy a pole supplied with different types of top kit – a match kit for small fish and a power kit for carp and specimen-sized fish.

Elsewhere in this chapter we'll look at how you marry elastic choice to the size of fish you're fishing for. But for now remember that the higher the number rating given to elastic the stronger it is – a No 5 is ideal for roach, for example, while a No 18 is ideal for large carp. The lighter elastic will go in a match kit, the stronger elastic in the power kit.

Whichever kit you're elasticating the process is largely the same and the picture sequence below explains how you do it according to the best tutor you could have, four-times World Champion Bob Nudd.

How to elasticate your pole

The following sequence gives you the full story when it comes to elasticating a match kit with solid elastic and a carp kit with strong hollow elastic. Don't be put off by the number of steps – it's a simple process and covers *everything* you need to know.

FITTING THE BUSH

1 To begin, cut back the tip section and fit the bushes to act as a buffer between the pole and the elastic. You need the elastics you're going to use, Liquid Weld industrial superglue, suitable pole bushes for the elastic you're going to use and a needle file.

2 Select the correct bush diameter for the size of elastic you're using. To begin I'm going to elasticate a match kit with a solid No 5 elastic, so a 1.27mm bore bush is ideal. The elastic should be a neat fit for the bush – snug without sticking – as this will stop water flooding inside the pole tip.

3 The tip of your top kit will be too thin for the bush to fit properly. You must cut it back until it grips the tip.

A key piece of advice is to cut the tip with a needle file, not a hacksaw. Saws tear at the carbon and splinter it whereas a fine needle file cuts it neatly. A set of needle files costs just a couple of pounds; make the investment – it can save you from a disaster.

4 Cut back a bit at a time and test the bush to see if it fits snugly. If you ~~d~~o it carefully the bush should be too ~~t~~ight to fit.

5 Cut off a little bit more and repeat the bush fitting until it fits tightly inside the tip. This is called an internal bush, as it goes inside the tip – this is preferred with light elastics.

6 Smooth off the edges with a fine needle file.

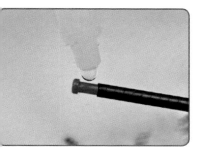

7 Fit the bush but don't push it all the way in – dab it with a blob of glue ~~a~~nd then push it the rest of the way.

8 Wipe away the excess glue to leave you with a snug-fitting bush that won't budge.

9 For a wide-bore carp kit follow the same cutting-back procedure as above to ensure that the bigger bush fits neatly. With heavy elastics an external bush that covers the outside of the pole section is better, as it doesn't restrict the diameter of the tip.

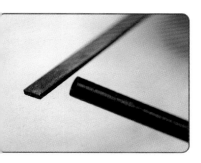

10 Once you've got a neat fit chamfer the edge of the carbon ~~w~~ith a fine needle file. It's common to ~~d~~iscard the whole of the number one ~~s~~ection when fitting a carp elastic so ~~t~~he bush often fits straight on to the ~~n~~umber two section.

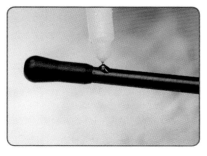

11 Push the bush on a little way, blob the pole with glue and push the bush right on. Wipe away the excess glue.

12 Here's the fine-bore match kit fitted with internal bush (left), and the carp kit with a large diameter external bush (right).

FITTING THE BUNG AND SOLID ELASTIC

Now that you've attached the bush it's time to fit the elastic itself. To do this you've got to start by fitting the bung that the elastic will be anchored to.

13 This is the kit you need – small and large bungs, hacksaw, elastics, diamond eye elastic threader, scissors and elastic connectors.

14 Cut back the bung before you run elastic through the pole. Like most brands these Browning bungs are available in different diameters to fit carp and match kits. Push the bung into the base of the top kit and mark where it stops with a pen.

15 Position the hacksaw blade 5mm above the mark. This is three or four steps up the bung.

16 Hacksaw through the bung, effectively reducing its diameter.

17 Use a bung extractor rod to push the bung into the top kit. It should go 6–7in (15–18cm) inside the section so that when the next section is pushed in it doesn't hit it.

18 To elasticate a match kit with fine elastic slide the diamond eye wire threader into the tip and shake it down until it comes out at the other end.

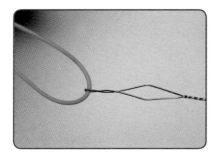

19 Slide the elastic through the eye on the threader.

20 If you're using fine elastic rated six or less, tie an overhand knot in it to stop it sliding out of the wire loop.

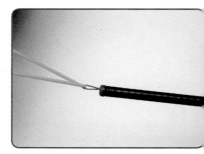

21 Pull the wire to drag the elastic into the tip and through the top two sections. When you're using a match kit with light elastic you only run it through the number one and two sections.

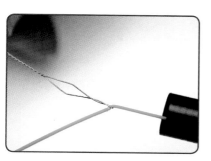

22 The knot will have slid up to the loop as you pulled the elastic through. Snip it off.

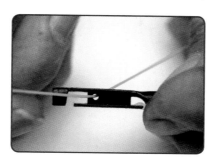

23 Put the elastic through the small hole on the end of the bung.

24 For a solid elastic, form a normal overhand knot (hollow elastic needs a different knot that I'll show you later).

25 Pull the elastic loop to partially close the knot *but don't fully tighten it*.

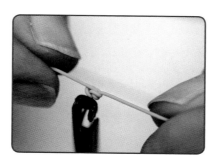

26 Ease your knot down to the top of the bung.

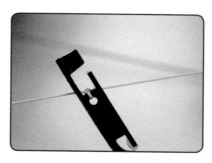

27 Pull both ends of the elastic to fully tighten it. The coils of elastic actually bite into each other and form a vice-like grip.

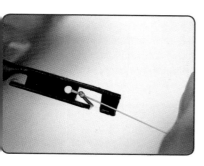

28 Trim off the tag end to form a neat knot on the connector and give the elastic a final tug to make sure it doesn't slip.

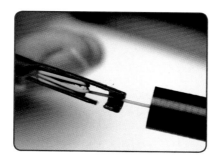

29 The Browning bungs have a winder section to hold extra elastic – wrap six turns around the winder, thread the elastic through the runner on the top of the bung and push it into the pole.

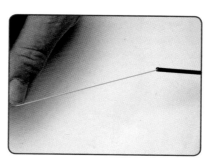

30 Now grab the elastic coming out of the tip and give it a few good stretches. New elastic is extra stretchy and it helps to take out this softness.

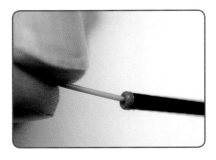

31 You now need to decide where to tie the rig connector. Pinch the laccy and pull it – you need to attach the connector at a point where the elastic pulls back smoothly into the pole.

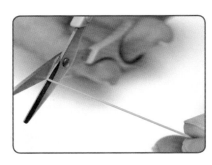

32 Once you've found the spot where the tension in the elastic smoothly pulls it back into the pole, cut it.

33 Get a mini connector that's suitable for using with fine lines and light elastic and slide the bottom sleeve section on to the elastic.

34 Now put the elastic through the hole in the bottom of the top section of the connector.

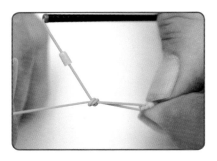

35 Tie an overhand knot in the elastic the same as was used to attach the bung, but *don't pull it tight*.

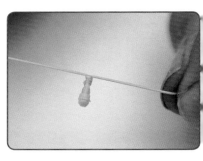

36 Ease the knot down to the connector and pull both ends to fully tighten it and nail it to the connector.

37 Trim the tag close to the knot to neaten it and ensure that the connector sleeve easily passes over the knot.

38 Slide the connector sleeve down to cover the knot.

39 The sleeve should double-click into place to stop the collar on top of the connector slipping when you hook a fish. A badly fitted connector is a common cause for lost fish.

40 Test the elastic tension by pulling it and letting go. It should pull back smoothly into the tip. If it snaps back hard or is floppy and doesn't pull back into the tip you need to alter the tension.

41 Use the bung extractor to remove the bung and wind more elastic on to it to increase the tension, or unravel some laccy to release the tension.

FITTING HOLLOW ELASTIC TO A CARP KIT – THE DIFFERENCES

Hollow elastic has one great advantage when you're pole fishing for carp – the extra stretch it provides is far better at absorbing the power of the fish and ensures you land more of them.

While it isn't good when you're fishing up to snags like lilies (the extra stretch helps big fish reach sanctuary), in open water situations 10–20 rated hollow elastics can't be beaten. However, there are a few subtle differences you need to note about elasticating a pole with hollow laccy.

42 For a start you don't need a diamond eye threader – the weight of the elastic allows you to drop it into the tip section and shake it through.

43 The bung and connector are attached with a different knot to that used with solid elastic. To show you how to tie it, here's how you attach the connector. First thread the laccy through the connector sleeve.

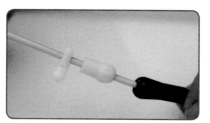

44 Thread the top section of the connector on to the elastic. As with the match kit, the size of the connector should match the thickness of the elastic and be a snug fit.

45 Wrap three turns of the elastic tag end round the elastic coming out of the pole tip.

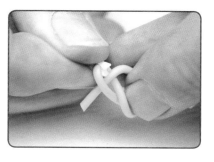

46 Tuck the end of the elastic through the hole directly beneath the connector.

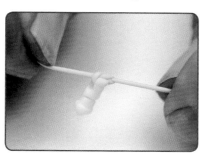

47 Pull the knot really tight to make it small enough for the connector sleeve to push over the knot.

48 Hollow elastic is quite thick and can make bulky knots that would stop the connector slotting together neatly, but this type of knot tightens down well.

49 If you've tied the knot well there will be no bulky pieces of elastic sticking out of the connector.

50 A well-tied connector sits square to the pole tip in the perfect position to have the rig attached to it.

Now for rig tying ...

So, you've got your pole, a number of key accessories to use with it, and you've elasticated the pole so that it's ready to use. All you've got to do now is set up a pole rig and you're ready to go fishing. So next we'll take a look at pole float designs and the types of shot you put on your rig. We can then show you how to tie a rig at home and store it on a winder ready to take to the bank.

Shotting up a pole rig

In the float fishing chapter we looked at round split shot, comparing different sizes and showing you how to put them on the line and how to use the correct loading for the shotting capacity marked on the side of the float. Well, the same basic rules apply for pole fishing too, but you'll find a few subtle differences.

The most obvious difference between pole and float set-ups is the size of the shot used and the total loading applied to the line, because a pole float is lowered into the water rather than being cast like a waggler float. Consequently there's no need to use a large float carrying a large casting weight to help propel the rig.

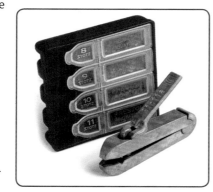

Pole floats are far more delicate than a normal waggler float, so they take a fraction of the shotting capacity. Rather than bulking large weights immediately under the float when you set up a pole rig, small shot are usually used and they're spread out through the length of the rig.

Although small sizes of traditional round split shot can certainly be used, different types of tiny shot are also available that make the fine-tuning of pole rigs far easier.

To avoid any confusion as you learn pole fishing skills here's a guide to what types of shot are available, how they're used and what they weigh. Remember, any shot larger than a No.8 (0.06g) up to 1oz (28.35g) must be made of non-toxic material rather than lead. If you're caught using illegal sizes of lead shot in the UK you could face a £5,000 fine, so don't do it!

Split shot

Round or egg-shaped with a central split cut into it. The line is slipped into the slot and the shot is squeezed until it grips the nylon. This is the classic type of shot used to shot a float rig. For pole fishing

you'll need small 'dust' shot between sizes 11 and 8.

Olivette

This is the largest type of weight that's used on heavy-duty pole rigs when fishing in rivers or very deep water, where you want to 'bomb' the hookbait quickly to the bottom.

Olivettes are streamlined weights that are threaded on to

the line so that the nylon runs straight through the weight or is pinned to its outside by rubber sleeves. They're available in sizes from 0.3g to 12g but aren't needed in most still-water fisheries with a depth of 7ft (2m) or less.

Styl

This long, thin, barrel-shaped weight was designed by Continental anglers to allow fine tuning of very delicate pole rigs. Styls are available in very small sizes

and allow the rig to fall through the water slower than comparable sizes of round shot.

They can be fiddly to attach to the line and aren't often used by the majority of pole anglers in the UK. However, many pole floats have their shotting capacity stated in styl weights, so it's necessary to know what these weights are (see the table right).

Stotz

The Stotz is a shorter, fatter version of the styl and is

marketed by Preston Innovations. Much easier to place on the heavier lines used in modern fisheries where large fish like carp dominate, they have a much wider groove cut in them. Available in sizes 8 to 13, the pictures here show how they're attached and removed. They're brilliant for quick and accurate shotting of pole rigs.

A guide to styl weights

Continental styl weights are classified in reverse compared to split shot – in other words, the higher the number the larger the shot. Lead styls from No.12 to No.20 are illegal in the UK.

No.7 = 0.01g
No.8 = 0.017g
No.9 = 0.025g
No.10 = 0.035g
No.11 = 0.048g

POLE FLOAT CONVERSION CHART

As explained above, despite styl weights no longer being popular many pole floats still have their shotting capacity stated in terms of the number of styls needed to shot it properly. This can cause massive confusion for novice pole anglers.

The list below provides an easy-to-follow styl weights to standard split shot conversion table:

3 x 10 styls = 0.1g (equivalent to two No 10 split shot)
4 x 10 styls = 0.15g (equivalent to three No 9 split shot)
4 x 12 styls = 0.2g (equivalent to five No 10 split shot)
4 x 14 styls = 0.4g (equivalent to six No 8 split shot)
4 x 16 styls = 0.5g (equivalent to eight No 8 split shot)
4 x 18 styls = 0.75g (equivalent to three No 3 split shot)

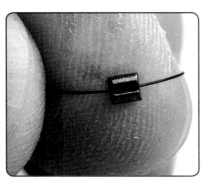

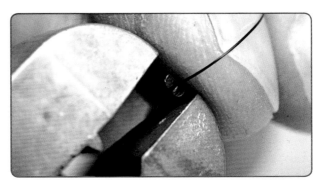

Drop the line into the slot in the Stotz.

Use the Stotta pliers to pinch the Stotz on to the line.

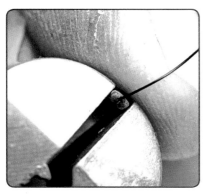

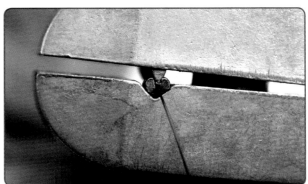

Don't squeeze too hard – a gentle pressure is enough.

Stotta pliers can also remove the Stotz from the line.

Know your floats

There are hundreds of different patterns of pole float available and it can be a huge source of confusion for budding pole anglers. The huge variety of body shapes, colours and materials they're made from is to allow float patterns to perform a host of tasks in a variety of different venues, from shallow lakes to fast-flowing rivers.

However, in this manual we aim to make fishing easy to understand so we'll give you a simplified guide to the four main shapes of pole float that you're likely to need in most situations.

1 Fat-bodied

Used in slow-moving rivers, as its pronounced shoulder and broad, buoyant body allows the user to hold the float back slightly against the flow of the water. This gives the angler more control over the speed at which the float travels downstream.

The bigger the float and the fatter the body the more buoyant it is and the faster/deeper the water it can be used in. Its thick, long and very buoyant tip also helps it ride the current.

2 Slim

The slender profile of this float makes it very responsive to bites, and very little shot is used to make it sit upright in the water. A short float with little buoyancy, it's ideal for use in very shallow water or for fishing up-in-the-water when fish are taking baits as they sink.

3 Dibber

A very short, fat and buoyant float that's ideal for fishing in very shallow water. Because of the length of the float it sits upright in the water instantly and is more inconspicuous.

Some anglers with poor eyesight also find that the fatter tip on a dibber is easier to see than the very slender cane or fibre tips generally used in pole floats.

4 Oval

This is probably the most popular design and is ideal for modern commercial still waters and natural lakes. In larger sizes it's often called a 'rugby ball-shaped' float as the body gets bigger and fatter!

The oval's slender body shape tapers down into a thin tip which makes it very responsive, so that it shows up bites very well and will register the drop of the shot attached to the line too. The fatter and larger the body is, the more buoyant the float will be and the more shot you'll need to add to the line.

Floats with shotting capacities of 0.1 to 0.6g (3 x 10 to 4 x 16 styls) will suit most lakes.

Making a pole rig

The rig you use on the end of your pole should be tied at home and stored on a special plastic winder until you want to use it. Not only does this ensure that you tie the very best rig you can (as it can be difficult to tie a delicate rig outside if it's windy), but making your rig at home also maximises your fishing time, since it means you don't have to set up a rig when you get to the waterside.

The picture sequence below shows how Bob Nudd ties a rig and then stores it on a winder ready for use…

1 Start by checking the size of the float capacity and select shot or an olivette slightly less than that figure. For a float over 0.5g use an olivette.

2 Push the olivette on to the base of the float stem so you can test the shotting load – they're so delicate that they can be slightly incorrect.

3 Invest in a testing tank such as a tall pasta jar. Fill it with water.

4 Lower the float into the water.

5 You want a fraction of the float body standing proud of the water – this is what the dropper shot will dot down.

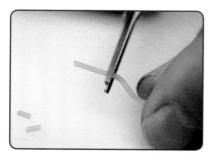

6 Cut two short pieces of micro-diameter silicone rubber pole tubing and one slightly longer piece. This tubing comes in different diameters so ensure that yours grips the stem of the float firmly.

7 Thread the mainline you're going to make the rig from through the eye on the pole float.

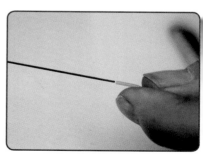

8 Thread the three pieces of silicone tube on to the opposite end of the mainline and slide them down to the float.

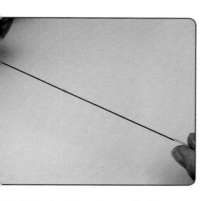

9 Slide the three pieces of tubing on to the float stem, one at the base of the body, one halfway down the stem, and the longer piece overhanging the end of the stem.

10 Thread the olivette on the line.

11 Browning olivettes are wedged in place with a tiny carbon bristle that's plugged into the silicone tubing running through the middle of the olivette.

12 In this example there's 0.1g of the float's shotting capacity to add. This means you can add three No.11 split shot or Stotz.

13 Use spring-loaded long-nose pliers to attach the shot to the line – it's easier and healthier than using your teeth!

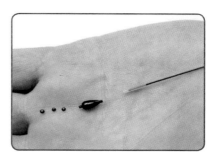

14 The olivette and dropper shot are now placed near the end of the line just below the float.

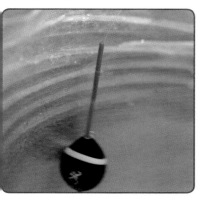

15 Put the float back in the testing tank and tweak the shot on the line until you get it to sit like this, with half the bristle showing.

16 Slide the float and shot up the line and snip off the piece where the shot was pinched, to avoid using damaged line.

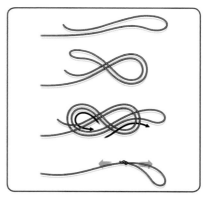

17 Use the figure-of-eight knot to put a loop in the end of the line then attach a hooklink with the loop-to-loop knot.

Storing a rig ready for use

Now that you've tied your rig you've got to store it ready for use. This means putting it on a rig winder. Here's how you do it…

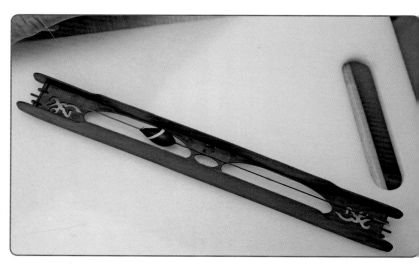

1 Make sure the winder is long and deep enough so that the float doesn't overhang it.

2 If the tip or body sticks out like this it will get broken.

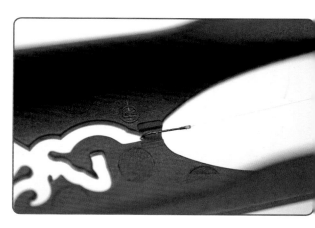

3 Slip the hook into one of the special holes cut in the winder body first. Then wrap the line round the winder.

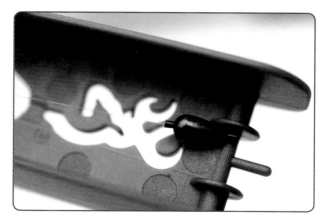

4 Ensure the split shot or olivette isn't wrapped around the end of the winder – this can knock the shot off the line or damage the monofilament.

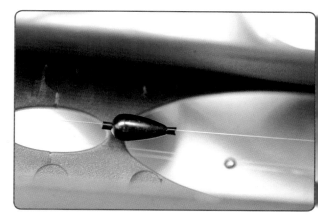

5 The shot should be on the line in the centre section of the winder.

6 Attach a soft rubber pole anchor to the loop in the end of the pole rig.

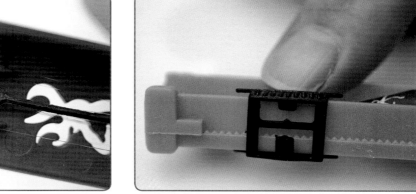

7 Slip the other end of the anchor over the peg on the end of the winder.

8 Some winders don't need a pole anchor thanks to this sliding device that holds the rig loop.

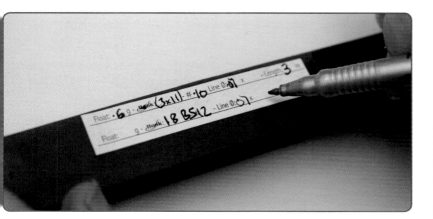

9 Attach a sticker to the side of the winder and write in the full details of the rig. Include the shotting capacity of the float, the line diameter and breaking strain, the hook size and the length of the rig.

Extra tips ...

So that's the rig tied, and you're almost ready to hit the waterside! Before you do, though, you first need to consider a few key things that can influence how well you fish. Over the page are six tips to point you in the right direction…

Balancing your tackle

In the same way that your line and hook needs to be balanced against the strength of your rod and the size of fish you're looking to catch when float and feeder fishing, so you need to strike a balance when pole fishing.

The strength of the hook, line, pole elastic and pole section must match each other. For example, if the elastic is too powerful for the line it'll snap very easily, if the elastic is too soft for the size of fish you're hooking you'll never get the upper hand and bring it into the net. A big fish will simply swim off and the elastic will not possess enough

resistance to sap its strength and bring it back to the bank.

Remember, the larger the number rating given to the elastic the thicker and stronger it is and, as with float and feeder fishing, the mainline above the hooklink should be made of slightly stronger line so that you don't lose your entire rig if the line gets snagged or a big fish picks up your bait and manages to snap the line. Think of the hooklink as a slightly weak point in your rig so that if a disaster occurs you only lose the hook and the last few inches of line.

The guide below shows you how to get the balance right.

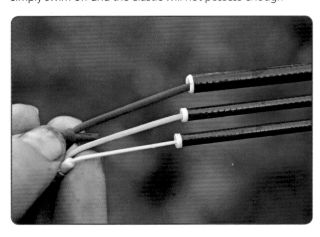

Elastic strength	Hooklink	Hook size	Target species
1 to 3	12oz to 1lb	22 to 24	Bleak, gudgeon
4 to 6	1.5lb to 3lb	18 to 20	Roach, small bream and perch
8 to 10	3.5lb to 4lb	12 to 18	Small (1–4lb) carp, bream, tench, chub
12 to 14	4.5lb to 5lb	12 to 18	Carp (4–6lb), large bream and tench
16 to 18	5.5lb to 8lb	10 to 14	Carp (6–10lb), big tench, barbel
20 to 24	8.5lb to 10lb	8 to 12	Big carp (10lb plus), barbel

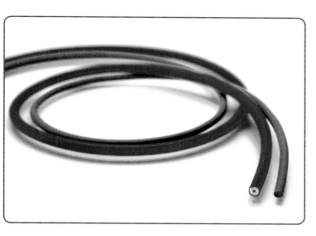

Hollow or solid?

The most basic type of elastic is solid all the way through. Tough and hard-wearing, they're colour coded by each manufacturer according to their thickness and strength. This helps you recognise which strength of elastic is fitted to which top kit so that you don't mistakenly pair your line and hook with the wrong strength of laccy. Solid elastics are also the cheapest option, so they're a great choice when you start pole fishing.

Hollow elastics, on the other hand, have a hollow core, which makes them stretch a lot more. They contract faster and more smoothly than traditional solid elastic and are also more expensive, and because they're stretchier they often have a rating that covers a range of strengths, such as 5 to 8 or 10 to 16.

Lubricate your elastic

To ensure that the elastic slips smoothly in and out of the pole you can also drip lubricant on it to make it more slippery. A few drops of lube (below) before you fish is all you need to keep the elastic running smoothly.

Protect your pole

The number three and four sections of a pole are repeatedly shipped and unshipped whenever you catch a fish or bring a rig in to re-bait it, and it's all too easy to hit the edges of the

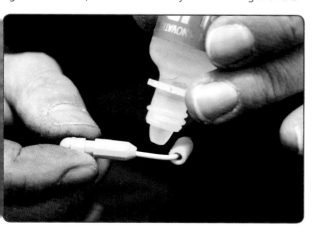

sections against each other, which can easily crack and splinter the carbon. Replacement sections can be very expensive.

So to protect your pole fit foam plugs, called Maver Clean Caps. They're a tight fit, so work them in your fingers to soften them and

then fit them in the base of the number three and four sections.

On the fatter sections that tend to be dropped or pushed along the floor fit a bigger foam plug, such as a Maver Shipper Bung, to cover the carbon edge of the section.

Test the elastic

Before you fish you need to test the tension of your elastic – too soft and you'll struggle to set the hook in the fish, too tight and you might bounce the fish off the hook.

Pinch the connector and pull the elastic out 8–10in (20–25cm), then let go of it. It should instantly zip back inside the pole quickly and smoothly. If it snakes slowly back into the pole you need to lubricate and tension the elastic some more by winding more elastic on to the winder bung as shown earlier. On the other hand, if the connector slams back against the pole bush, hitting it with an audible 'crack', it's too tight and the tension needs to be reduced.

Get catching ...

Right, you've set up your pole and tied some rigs ready to catch fish. Now we're ready to get you pole fishing. So let's head to the lake and we'll show you how to set up your tackle and get you catching fish.

Setting up for pole fishing

How you set yourself up on the bank of the fishery is vital to becoming a successful pole angler, yet it's something that almost every newcomer does incorrectly. In fact lots of very experienced anglers get this bit dreadfully wrong too, and suffer the consequences.

How you sit by the water, hold the pole and ship it in and out is important. Do it wrong and you can be very uncomfortable and even suffer back and shoulder pain. This will spoil your fishing and make you fish poorly. But if you follow the simple guidelines below you'll set up your seat box properly, fish in comfort all day long and thoroughly enjoy your day by the water.

1 Place your box on the peg a couple of feet back from the water's edge.

2 A footplate is a great accessory – if your box has an integral one slide it out. If it isn't supplied with a footplate it's a good idea to fit one.

3 Use the box's adjustable leg system to level the box and footplate.

4 Stand on the footplate – the crease of your knee should be an inch above the seat cushion.

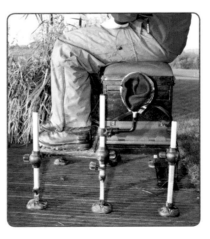

5 When seated, your feet, knees and back should all be at 90° angles. This stops you straining your muscles.

6 Attach a large side tray to the leg system on the opposite side of the box to where you'll hold the pole. I'm a left-hander so you'll need to reverse the directions if you're right-handed!

7 This tray holds your bait and essential items of tackle such as disgorger, plummet and split shot.

8 A pole sock is attached to the front seat box leg on the side where you'll hold the pole.

9 A pole roller is placed behind and slightly to the side of your seat box. This helps you ship the pole backwards and forwards and supports the pole as you do so.

10 The pole should be placed so that it's balanced as it comes off the roller – it shouldn't drop like this, as the rig will be bounced and tangles will be caused.

11 Don't place the roller too far away or the pole will sag like this. This puts extra strain on the pole and may break the sections.

12 Also don't place the roller too near to you or the pole will droop on the other side, which could cause breakages.

13 When the pole has been shipped in and the top kit has been unshipped for a fish to be landed or the rig re-baited, slide the end section of the pole into the sock. This anchors the pole supported on the roller and stops it blowing away and getting damaged.

14 When you've baited your rig attach the top kit to the rest of the pole and drop the rig in the margins of the lake.

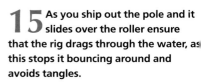

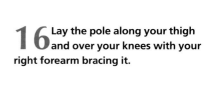

15 As you ship out the pole and it slides over the roller ensure that the rig drags through the water, as this stops it bouncing around and avoids tangles.

16 Lay the pole along your thigh and over your knees with your right forearm bracing it.

17 Your feet are flat on the footplate and your knees are bent at 90°, as is your back.

18 This is the perfect posture, as the weight of the pole is evenly distributed through your legs, arms and back.

The rigs you need ...

Now it's time to go fishing, and here are two basic rigs that'll see you catch fish in most situations. .

Follow the directions on how to tie a pole rig given on page 122, and this diagram will give you the rest of the information you need to construct great rigs.

As you become more proficient at pole fishing other more complicated set-ups will be added to your armoury, but to start with these set-ups will cover most fisheries and will catch you an awful lot of fish.

Use very small slender floats of 0.1–0.2g when fishing up-in-the-water. Line and elastic strength and hook size are dictated by the size of fish you are catching (see the table on page 126).

These tiny floats carry very small amounts of shot. Use two or three No.8 or 10 shot, one just below the float, the other spread down the foot or two of line to the hook.

Most anglers fish without a hooklink and prefer to tie the hook direct to the line. This helps with the natural fall of the hookbait.

When fishing on the bottom you can use the same rig for big or little fish. The only difference is the balance of line, hook and elastic strength (see page 126).

Increase the float size by 0.1g per foot of water – a 0.6g float is ideal for a six feet deep swim. Place the shot required in the bottom third of the rig with a bulk of shot and one or two No.8 or 10 droppers below.

The hookbait is set dead-depth or up to two inches over-depth if the float is being dragged by any undertow.

The up-in-the-water rig

The big difference with this set up (above left) compared to the multi-purpose bottom rig opposite is that after plumbing has been completed this rig has been set to present the bait in the top couple of feet of water.

Designed to catch fish that are feeding high in the water column, this rig is ideal for catching carp and silverfish.

Once again the components used are balanced to the size of fish you're trying to catch. Rigs like this can catch lots of silverfish in some waters or they can tempt really big carp in other waters.

As with all types of fishing, you need to do some homework on the fishery you are going to fish to make sure you set up with the right kit that can cope with the fish you'll catch.

The key thing with using an up-in-the-water rig is the ability to loosefeed regularly and accurately so the hookbait is constantly dropping through a cloud of freebies (see page 136 for details on how to feed while holding the pole).

This is an all-action style of fishing where you should lift and drop the rig every 30–60 seconds to give the hookbait a fresh drop through the water. Once it has fully sunk and is unnaturally hanging in mid-water, fish will be far more reluctant to take it.

The multi-purpose bottom fishing rig

Careful plumbing has allowed this rig to be set up so that the hookbait comes to rest just touching the bottom – this is called 'dead-depth' fishing.

As it has been designed to fish at full depth, most of the shot have been spaced out in the bottom third of the rig. This will give your hookbait a slow and natural descent to the lakebed, especially in the last couple of feet, where a lot of fish shoal up.

Bites will often come before the float has fully settled, so be ready for bites coming as the float settles. In fact, if a fish takes the bait as it drops, the float may not settle at all as a fish is holding up some of the shot. This is just as much a sign of a bite as the float going under so strike straight away.

Depending on the size of fish you're after you'll need to decide on the balance of line, hooks and elastics (see page 126).

If you're after small fish you'll need a match top kit loaded with light number 5/6 elastic and 2–4lb lines to suit. To beef up the rig to cope with carp, pick a slightly tougher float, use a power top kit loaded with strong elastic and gear up the line to 5–8lb.

Plumbing for pole fishing

In the same way that plumbing the depth of the water is vital to accurately setting up a waggler float rig, so it is equally important when setting up a pole rig.

On the previous pages we've shown you rigs for fishing at different depths, so to ensure you select the right rig here's a guide to how you measure and record the depth of water in your swim when pole fishing.

The good news is that because you lower a pole rig into the water directly below the tip, plumbing up is even easier than with the waggler float, and it's possible to map the lake bed very accurately. Working the plummet across the swim and at different distances from the bank you'll soon be able to register changes in depth and locate some vital fish-holding features.

Plumbing up is the essential legwork that sets you up for a successful pole fishing session. Here's how you do it:

1 Attach the rig you've made at home to the pole connector. The sleeve is pushed back, the loop on the top of the rig is slipped on and the sleeve is pushed back to lock the rig in place.

2 Unravel the rig from the winder and thread the hook through the loop on the top of a large plummet.

3 Push the hook into the cork strip or the base of the plummet. Make a best guess at the depth of the water and position the float accordingly.

4 Ship out to the spot you intend to fish and lower the rig into the water. You'll be able to feel the heavy plummet sink through the water and hit the bottom.

5 If your float stands out of the water like this as the plummet hits the bottom, the rig is a few inches over-depth and you need to slide it down the line.

6 If the float is pulled under the surface by the plummet the rig is set under-depth and needs to be slid up the line.

7 In this photo around 5mm of the float tip is visible as the plummet touches down. This is a fraction over 'dead depth', and you know exactly how deep the water is.

8 Detach the plummet and pull the hook down to the bottom of the nearest pole section. Slip the hook over the end of the pole to pull the rig tight.

9 Use a white chinagraph pencil (available from stationery shops) to mark the position of the float. This records the water depth so that you can then decide where to place your hookbait. It also means you can instantly set a new rig to the right depth if you have to re-tackle.

Advanced tips for pole success

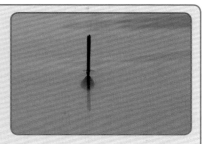

1 Many modern poles have special alignment arrows marked on them. Not only do they number the sections to ensure that you know which ones fit together, but if you line up the arrows on each section the pole will maintain the best action.

2 You don't have to fish at one depth all day. Top anglers such as Kieron Rich often alter the depth they fish in order to catch mixed bags. Different species often feed at different depths so experiment with rigs set to fish at 'dead depth' and half-depth.

3 How low you dot the float down affects its sensitivity – the more the float tip sticks out of the water the more buoyant it will be and the harder it will be for fish to pull it under. A float dotted like this will take more pulling under but might be good if lots of large carp are bumping into your rig, as the float won't get pulled under by line bites.

4 By dotting down the pole float so that only a small amount of tip is showing it will be easy for fish to pull it under. This picture shows an ideal position for most fishing situations – there's just under half a centimetre standing proud of the water.

5 If you're fishing for shy-biting species such as crucian carp you might need to dot down the float even more until just a pimple of tip is showing. As long as your eyes are good enough to see it this will be super-sensitive. A fish only needs to mouth the bait for the float to go under.

6 Top angler Russ Evans dotted his rig right down to help him register interest from these fine crucians. These notoriously shy-biting fish will often give the most delicate bites and a sensitive pole rig is the best way to catch them.

The importance of feeding

No matter which one of the rigs we've shown you choose to use, the importance of loosefeeding is crucial – if you don't regularly and accurately feed around your float you will catch fewer fish.

There are four main feeding techniques you can use for pole fishing, and it's essential that you master them all.

Pole cupping

A 'pole cup' is screwed on to the end of the special cupping kit supplied with many pole packages. Groundbait and loosefeed is placed inside the cup, shipped out to the spot you want to fish, and the pole is then rotated to drop its contents in the water.

It's great for quickly laying down a carpet of feed and is often used at the start of a fishing session to lay a foundation for the day ahead. It's also a good way of feeding a large quantity of food at the same time, which helps in

getting loosefeed past the hordes of very small fish that can fill the upper layers of many lakes.

In the warmer months, when fish are feeding strongly, it's a good tactic to put in half a cup-load of pellets or a ball or two of groundbait before you even get started.

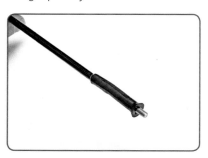

1 Many poles are supplied with a cupping kit complete with a screw fitting like this.

2 The pole cup is then screwed on when you want to feed your swim.

3 Balls or nuggets of groundbait can be placed in the cup, shipped out to the spot you want to fish and dropped in the water.

4 Crumbly groundbait can also be trickled into the pole cup.

5 The crumb can then be tipped into the water to create a cloud of feed that cascades down to the bottom.

Pole potting

A pole pot is a miniature baiting cup that's fixed to the top kit you're fishing with. Loosefeed is put into it prior to the rig being shipped out, and once your rig is in position it's a simple task to rotate the pole and tip the bait near the float with pinpoint accuracy.

Open grooves are located on the base of the pot to allow it to be placed over the end of the tip section. The pot is then slid down the end section until it grips the carbon.

Pole potting is arguably the most effective feeding tactic there is, and it's essential that every budding pole angler should master it. Cheap and very effective, you *must* kit yourself out with a set of pole pots to fit your top kits. Some are made with wide grooves in them to fit powerful carp kits while others have narrower slots to fit smaller bore match kits.

1 A variety of different sizes of pole pot are available.

2 This Fox pot is typical of many designs. A couple of slots are formed in the base and these fit over the end of the pole tip.

3 The pot is then slid a few inches down the tip until the thicker diameter grips the pot.

4 Loosefeed such as corn and pellets can be dropped into the pot. Note the lip on this pot to prevent spillage.

5 Mini baits like maggots and casters can also be potted.

6 Fine fishmeal groundbait can be sprinkled into the pot and gently tamped down to stop it spilling as you ship out the rig.

7 When the rig is in position rotate the pole and tap it with the palm of your hand to dislodge the nugget of groundbait right round your float.

Catapulting

Feeding with a catapult while holding the pole isn't an easy art to master, but it's a key skill that's particularly effective if you're fishing up-in-the-water with a short rig for catching fish near the surface.

When you're trying to tempt fish high in the water the sight and sound of loosefeed hitting the water is a key feeding trigger – so if you can catapult a pinch of bait round your float every minute or two you'll draw the fish towards your hookbait and will catch a lot more than if you can't feed while your rig is in the water. This sequence shows England international Des Shipp feeding with a catapult:

1 Loosefeeding with a catapult can help you catch more fish as they respond to the sight and sound of feed hitting the water near your float.

2 Des Shipp is an expert at feeding with the catapult while holding the pole.

3 Roach like this cracker often respond to the arrival of catapulted loosefeed.

4 Brace the pole across your thighs and under your right forearm (reverse these directions if you're left-handed).

5 Position your catapult and bait on the tray on the left-hand side of the box. Pick up the catty with your left hand.

6 Put the frame of the catapult in your right hand, grab a pinch of bait with your left and load it into the pouch.

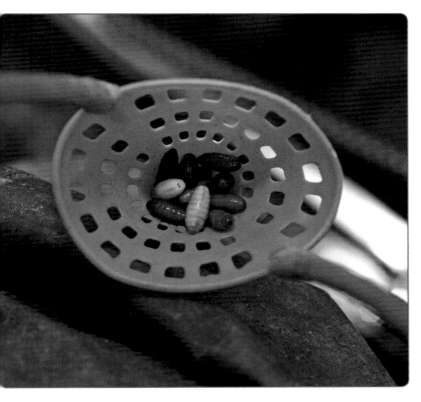

8 Grab the catapult frame with your left hand and swing the pouch tag into your right hand. Push the frame forward to load the correct amount of tension into the elastic to fire baits near the float.

7 A pinch of casters sitting in the bottom of the catty pouch.

9 Release the grip on the pouch to send the bait flying out close to the float.

By hand!

It might seem obvious, but when you're margin pole fishing feeding by hand is the easiest and most effective way of boosting your peg. It takes just seconds to grab some bait and flick it close to the float or down the marginal vegetation on both margins of your swim.

Feeding by hand is very quick, but the distance you can reach effectively is limited. If you try to loosefeed most baits beyond 8m (25ft) or so you'll spread it out too much.

Big carp like this brute are often found feeding very close to the marginal vegetation in summer. Loosefeeding by hand is ideal when you're fishing at short range down the edge.

Catching fish on the pole

You now have all the information you need to set up a great pole rig and get your gear perfectly positioned on the waterside. Now lets look at how all this is brought together to catch a fish.

1 This is a typical commercial fishery with a mixed stock of fish and a depth of around 6ft (1.8m). Although there are plenty of different species in the lake carp are the dominant fish, so a 12 to 18 rated elastic and lines/hooks to suit are fitted to the pole.

2 The hookbait is a soft hooker pellet slipped on to the size 16 wide-gape hook and positioned in the bend (left).

3 A power top kit has been fitted to the pole to carry the strong elastic so a suitable pole pot has been attached. This is a Fox Mega Tip Toss Pot filled with a few feed pellets.

5 Once in position the rig is lowered into the water and the pole is rotated to drop the loosefeed next to the float. The pole is braced comfortably between thighs and forearm.

4 With the baited rig dropped in the water the pole is shipped out with the pole running on the roller and the rig dragging through the water to stop it tangling.

6 When the bite comes a sharp lift of the pole is all that's needed to set the hook into the fish taking the bait.

7 If the fish is a large one hold the pole low to the water and allow the elastic to stretch out. Let the elastic do the work rather than the pole. Don't pull back on the pole to bend it – instead allow the elastic to slide out at a slight angle to the hooked fish.

8 As it saps the strength of the fish and you feel the elastic start to relax ship the pole backwards and drop it on to the roller.

9 Push the pole along the roller while judging the resistance pulling on the elastic. If the fish sets off on another run ship out the pole and allow the elastic to stretch.

10 If the tension in the elastic slowly relaxes roll the pole backwards until you reach the top kit. Unship the pole at this joint and place the detached pole in the pole sock.

11 Use the pole kit and strong elastic to draw the fish towards the landing net.

12 Spread the load on the top kit by laying it along your forearm.

13 Sink the net and draw the fish over the net rim. If you feel the fish try to power off again drop the pole lower to the water to allow the elastic to stretch out again.

14 Eventually the elastic will do its job and fish like this beauty will be yours.

15 The pole is a great catcher of fish, big and small. Gear up with the right kit for the size of fish you're after and you will enjoy your pole fishing.

CARP FISHING

Essential kit for carping 142

Laying out your carp kit 146

Understanding carp rig materials 148

Tying a hooklink 152

How to make a coated braid hooklink 154

Putting together a lead clip 156

Putting together a running leger clip 158

Boilies – cutting through the confusion 160

Hookbaits to catch carp 162

Spot-on casting 165

Spodding – the accurate way to bait up 168

Landing, unhooking, weighing and releasing a carp 171

Specialist carp fishing is the big growth area in modern angling. Since the 1980s, when a revolution started in the tackle, rigs and baits used to catch large carp, the number of people who specialise in catching specimen-sized fish has grown every year.

This growth in popularity has also generated a dramatic change in fishery management, and a burgeoning number of lakes are now home to 10lb and 20lb-plus carp so that it's easier than ever before to get access to lakes holding big fish.

In this chapter we'll detail the baits, rigs and tactics that can get you consistently catching fish but to start with we'll look at the specialist tackle you need for this style of fishing.

Essential kit for carping

Picking your rod

The most obvious piece of kit you need is a specialist carp rod that's been designed to have the power to cast a baited rig a long way, and the strength to absorb the fight of a big fish and guide it into the landing net.

As with swimfeeder rods, different models of carp rod

Below: A strong rod is essential to launch a large leger when carping. A 12ft-long, 2.75lb to 3lb test curve rod is ideal.

have varying actions. Some are relatively soft and bend evenly throughout their length, others are beefed up with what's called a 'fast-taper' action – this means that the lower butt section is much stiffer than the tip in a bid to make the rod more powerful to aid long-range casting.

While a tackle dealer can help you pick a rod that has an action to suit your particular carp fishing needs, the most basic indicator of rod power is its 'test curve' rating. Often stated as 'TC' on the rod, this is a measurement of the weight that's needed to bend the tip through 90°. As a general rule the higher the rating, the stiffer and more powerful the rod is. For example, a 2lb test curve rod will not be as stiff or powerful as a 3lb test curve rod.

Lengths of rod can also vary between 11ft and 13ft. Again, the longer rod is usually used for more extreme long-range casting demands and will therefore tend to have a higher test curve and a stiffer action.

Although rods from different manufacturers do vary, as a general guide most anglers will require a 12ft rod with a test curve of 2.5lb, 2.75lb or 3lb.

If you're likely to spend most of your carp fishing sessions fishing at shorter ranges of 50m or less, the lower test curve rod is ideal – it'll have the added benefit of being more enjoyable to play specimen fish on because of its softer, springier action. On the other hand, if you're likely to be fishing at long range or you're going to try to catch particularly big fish, the higher test curve rod is more suitable, although it won't be so nice to play hooked fish on because it will be much stiffer.

In most cases a 12ft 2.75lb rod is ideal. Just make sure it has a good quality screw-down reel seat and strong, lined guides running down the rod.

A reel for casting and playing fish

A powerful rod that's used for landing big fish needs to be matched to a reel that has the 'guts' to suit.

Carp reels tend to be much larger than float or feeder reels – 6,000 to 8,000 size are most suited to carping, compared to 3,000 and 4,000 size for float and feeder fishing.

bove: Reels like this are ideal for carp fishing. A 6,000 size reel is uitable for most carp fishing situations.

Above: Larger 10,000 size 'big pit' reels are only really needed for long-range casting.

When choosing a carp reel you need to pick the brains of tackle dealer for advice. You want to get one with top uality bearings, gearing and a clutch system that's highly djustable, to release line smoothly when a big fish has been ooked and is being played. A carp reel will be asked to do a ot of heavy-duty work, as it will be required to repeatedly rank in heavy leger rigs and tame large, hard-fighting fish.

Another very useful feature which is found on many carp eels is a free-spool system, invented by Shimano, who oined the phrase 'Baitrunner'. These reels are fitted with a pecial drag system that allows a predetermined tension to e applied to the reel spool when a rig is cast out, and pplies resistance to a big carp that picks up and runs with our bait. This check on the fish slows it down and helps the ngler gain control of it at the start of a fight. The free spool an be disengaged with the turn of the reel handle when ou pick the rod up.

For long-range fishing particularly large 10,000 size nodels (often called 'big pit' reels) can be used, but in most ases a 6,000 or 8,000 size top quality reel will do the job, oaded with 12lb to 15lb breaking strain line (see pages 8/29 for details on loading a reel).

Below: The Shimano Baitrunner system was the pioneer, but lots of manufacturers now make similar free-spool systems. They're switched on by the flick of a lever.

Electronic fishing

One of the specialist types of kit most readily associated vith carp fishing is the bite alarm, designed to alert the angler o a bite. The line runs through the alarm and when a fish picks p the bait and 'runs' with it the movement in the line triggers n audible 'beep' and LED lights on the case illuminate.

Useful during daylight hours, bite alarms are especially

Above: Bite alarms are great for alerting you to a run, especially at night. The line is also clipped into a hanging bite indicator between the reel and the alarm to give you extra information on how a hooked fish is moving.

Above: A full-blooded run will see the alarm scream and the indicator will slam up to the rod as line is pulled off the reel.

Above: If the fish moves towards you with the bait the line goes slack, the indicator falls back and the alarm will sound.

valuable for fishing at night, as they allow the user to sleep while the rod continues to fish. The alarm and lights then wake the angler if a fish takes the bait.

Other specialist kit

A LARGE LANDING NET
When you're fishing for big fish you need a landing net that can swallow a specimen. A 36 to 42in diameter net is ideal.

A ROD POD
On many lakes anglers fish from wooden, concrete or gravel platforms and this can make it difficult to drive in a bankstick to support your rod rest. The solution is a 'rod pod', a stand-alone frame that can hold two or three rods complete with bite alarms and rod rests.

A RUCKSACK
A large rucksack is ideal for carrying your small bits of tackle and bait to the bank.

Above: A quality unhooking mat like this Nash Carp Cradle is essential to look after your catch. Place it near the rods so that you can easily place a landed fish in it.

Above: Forceps to safely remove the hook, and medicated solution to help a fish repair any wounds, will help you care for carp.

UNHOOKING MAT AND FORCEPS

Big carp need to be looked after carefully when they're landed, and a padded unhooking mat is essential. When a fish is banked it should be laid on the soft unhooking mat while the forceps are used to carefully remove the hook. The best designs of unhooking mat also have high sides to stop the fish sliding off.

BIVVY AND BEDCHAIR

If you intend to fish for carp by night – which is a very productive time of day on most fisheries – you'll need an all-weather bivvy tent, a bedchair to sleep on and a sleeping bag to keep you warm. A head torch is also essential to help you see what you're doing whilst keeping your hands free to perform tasks like baiting a rig or unhooking a fish.

Left: A solid bivvy like this Nash Titan will keep you dry even in bad weather, while a bedchair and sleeping bag will help you fish through the night in comfort.

Turn the page to see how this kit should be put together and laid out beside the water…

Laying out your carp kit

This photograph gives you a basic idea of how the main items of carp gear should be set up beside the water, especially if you're setting up a bivvy system in order to fish at night.

1 Rod and reel
The rod should ideally be set up to one side of the swim. This gives you space in the vacant part of the peg to play and land hooked fish. The rod rests should be placed so that the first rod ring is behind the bite alarm, with the rear rod rest sited behind the reel to stabilise the set-up.

2 Bite indicator
Between the bite alarm and rod rest you can attach a bite indicator that hangs on the line. If a carp makes off with your hookbait the line will move forward or back and you'll get an extra

indication of a bite in addition to the alert from the bite alarm.

Indicators like this are especially useful if the fish picks up the bait and runs back towards the angler. This releases tension in the line and the weight of the indicator ensures it falls back. This is called a 'drop-back bite'. Dayglow isotopes can be fitted into these indicators to help you read a bite at night.

3 Landing net
This should be set up in the open part of the swim ready to be used when a fish is hooked.

4 Bivvy
If space allows, this should be set up at the side of the rods so that it doesn't get in the angler's way when casting.

5 Bedchair
Inside the bivvy are the bedchair and sleeping bag, with all the

ey items of tackle within easy each. The head torch and scales re immediately to hand, hanging ff the ratchet of the bedchair.

Unhooking mat

he unhooking mat and forceps hould be on a flat piece of ground t the back of the swim, waiting to eceive a landed fish. Again, this houldn't hinder casting.

Chair

 chair is essential if you aren't ight fishing or you don't want to eep moving your bedchair out of he bivvy during daylight hours. The hair is placed at the side of the ods so that the angler can quickly espond to a bite and it doesn't get n the way of casting. The best nglers will use time sitting in the hair to scan the water for signs of sh activity, such as carp jumping r rolling on the surface. One ghting of a fish can pinpoint a reat place to cast a hookbait.

Cooking equipment

ou need to feed yourself if you're arp fishing, especially if you're taying overnight. A small camping as stove is ideal for making hot rinks and easy meals. Don't cook nside the bivvy, to avoid a build-up f fumes, and make sure the stove an't set fire to any other fabric.

Tackle box

 small tackle box is ideal for toring rig-making material, baiting eedles and hooklinks. Stow it nder the bedchair, where it's easily t hand.

0 Bait

ait and baiting equipment should e stored in a cool bag or rucksack, ut you must be able to get at them asily so that you can re-bait a rig uickly after catching a fish. Carp re shoal fish, so getting a fresh bait ack in the water quickly can get ou another bite. Consequently eing well organised on the bank elps you catch more fish.

Understanding carp rig materials

Walk into any tackle shop and you'll be hit by the sight of a myriad of boards displaying a baffling array of specialist rig-making components.

Providing a comprehensive guide to every one of these gadgets would necessitate a book in itself, so what we're going to do in this manual is to simplify the choice by highlighting the essential items you'll need and giving you a quick brief as to what job they do.

As you become an accomplished carper you may well buy more specialised pieces of rig-making kit, but to kick off your carp-fishing career you don't need to break the bank by buying a mass of products that you won't initially need. Pick wisely, spend your money cleverly and you'll soon be catching fish with the minimum of tackle.

Hooks

You need to pick a strong, sharp and reliable hook to land a big, hard-fighting carp. Size 10 to 6 hooks are required by regular carpers to match the size of the baits being used. Different patterns also feature different shapes of hook; the pictures below show long-shanked, wide-gape and curved-shank hooks.

There's no right or wrong choice – experience and experimentation will lead you to choose whichever shape works best for you – but in case you get baffled by the bewildering array of hooks facing you just make sure the one you pick is strong and sharp. Ideally it should also have a slightly turned-in eye.

Leger weight

Commonly called a lead, a leger is attached to the mainline to give you the required casting weight to reach the distance you want to fish. With many set-ups the leger is also used to automatically hook the carp when it picks up your bait.

Many different shapes and sizes of leger weight are available. As a general rule you should match the weight of lead you use to the test curve of your rod – *ie* a 2.5oz leger i

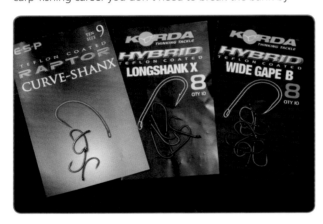

Above: Here are the three main types of carp hook; whichever you go for always change a hook as soon as the point shows any sign of wear. The sharper the hook the better it performs.

Below: Note how all three types of hook have a slightly inward-turned eye at the top of the shank. This helps a hook turn over and prick a fish that's picked up your bait.

Below: Different shapes of lead are available. Torpedo-shaped legers generally cast further but dumpy-shaped leads may be better for hooking fish, as they concentrate resistance in a smaller area. Most legers are now camouflaged. The Atomic Dung Bomb (right) i even covered in a compost-like material to make it less obvious to wary carp.

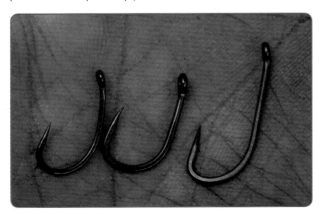

Above: Monofilament nylons like these are used as mainlines for your reel but can be used as hooklinks too.

Above: Braided line like this is super-thin and very strong.

good for a 2.5lb test curve rod, a 3oz leger is best for a 3lb test curve rod, and so on.

As for which shape of leger you pick, go for a pear-, square- or torpedo-shaped weight with a swivel built into the top. This helps you attach it to the rig.

Nylon

There are literally dozens of different hooklink materials available and the most traditional one for carp fishing is a strong nylon line. Typically lines of 10lb to 15lb are used for hooklinks. This type of nylon line is strong and abrasion resistant but is also stiff, which can make your hookbait behave unnaturally.

A special type of nylon has been created called fluorocarbon. Due to the high-tech materials used in its construction this is almost invisible in water, which may help to trick wary carp that refuse baits fished on cruder tackle. It's also very tough and stiff, which can affect how a hookbait behaves in water.

Braid

This modern material is made from a mass of superfine filaments that have been woven (or braided) into a single very thin and very strong line.

Much softer and thinner than nylon and fluorocarbon of

Right: There are dozens of different types of coated braid available.

a similar breaking strain, the main advantages of braided lines are that they allow a hookbait to move naturally and they can be camouflaged to match a particular colour of the lake bed. On the downside they can be more prone to tangles and aren't as tough or abrasion resistant as nylon.

Coated braid

This is something of a hybrid between nylon line and braid. At its core is a soft high-tech braid that's been coated with a layer of plastic. This makes the line thicker but it also makes it tougher and stiffer, which can help avoid tangles when casting. The coating can also be fractured or parts of it stripped away to allow the hookbait to move freely on the soft braided core.

Lead clips

One of the basic principles of most modern carp rigs is that they're 'self-hooking' – which means that the leger that's attached to the line to give you casting weight is also used to hook the carp when it picks up your hookbait.

On feeling the weight of the leger as it moves off with your bait in its mouth, the carp will react to the resistance by

Below: The plastic coating can be stripped away to reveal the softer braided core.

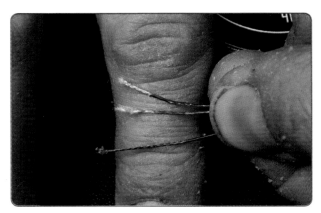

Left: Many off-the-shelf lead clip rigs are available. They're a great buy for novice and expert alike.

Below: The clip holds the leger for casting and self-hooking the carp when it picks up your bait. If the rig becomes snagged the leger can pull off the clip to stop the carp becoming snared.

charging off (this is why this type of rig is also known as a 'bolt rig') and the hook is automatically driven home.

A lead clip is simply a small plastic lug that allows the leger to be easily attached to the line and, just as importantly, allows the weight to be jettisoned if it's dragged into a bed of weeds, lilies or rushes by a big carp. This will help you land the fish. The ability to eject the leger weight also helps if the mainline above the clip snaps – this avoids a hooked fish having to drag the weight around and risk damaging itself. For this reason a lead clip rig is known as a 'semi-fixed' or 'safe' rig.

Running legers

A simple alternative set-up to the lead clip is the running leger rig.

Many kits are available that use a large-bore plastic ring, which is threaded on to the mainline and slides on the nylon above the hooklink. The leger weight is clipped on to this ring so that when a fish picks up the bait the line slides through the ring with minimal resistance.

This maximises bite registration and makes the rig extremely safe, as any breakage of the mainline will allow the leger weight to slide away and avoid a hooked carp having to pull it around.

Above: Ready-made kits like these are perfect for constructing running leger rigs.

Weighted leaders and rig tubing

Tangles are something every angler suffers at some time but these two products can greatly reduce the chance of your rig tangling on the cast or while being retrieved.

The weighted leader is a relatively new product but has made a big impact. The leader is a short section of heavy-duty, plastic-coated line that's tied to the mainline at one end and the hooklink at the other. The leger is also attached to the leader, which because it's thicker and stiffer than the mainline and hooklink reduces the likelihood of tangles.

Dots of tungsten underneath the coating pins down the leader near the hookbait to reduce the chance of a wary fish spotting it and being spooked. It also adds a short and very tough section of line just above the hooklink to provide extra strength and abrasion resistance. This is especially useful if a hooked fish charges into a bed of weed or rubs up against the branches of a sunken tree.

Rig tubing works in a similar fashion to a weighted leader except that it's hollow so that the mainline can be threaded through the tubing and tied to the top of the hooklink. Its primary job is to stiffen the line to reduce the chance of tangles.

Below: Spots of tungsten pin down a leader. Many companies now produce ready-made leaders that can be used off-the-shelf.

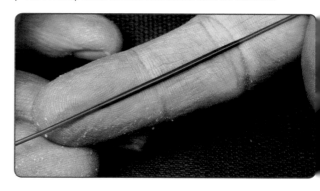

Above: Cheap but essential, these E-S-P boilie stops are great for holding a bait on the end of a hair rig.

Boilie stops

These small plastic barrels are simply used to hold the hookbait on the hair-rig loop hanging below the hook in every carp rig.

Baiting needles

Baits are threaded on to a baiting needle that's then attached to the hair rig so that the bait can be transferred from needle to hooklink.

Get one short, sharp needle for baiting the rig and one long-lip 'stringer needle', which is ideal for use with PVA.

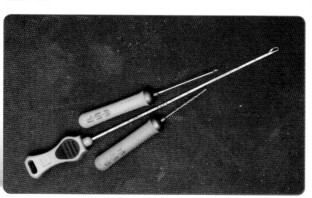

Above: You need three pieces of baiting equipment – a long stringer needle, a sharp fine bore baiting needle and a micro bait drill to help hair-rig hard baits like tiger nuts.

Left: A lip-close needle, fine drill bit and a fine and very sharp needle are needed for hair-rigging baits.

Right: PVA mesh/web is one of the most important aids to catching carp – you MUST learn how to use it.

Below: Different deniers of PVA mesh are available. Fine mesh is ideal for holding live baits like maggots and crumbled boilies or groundbait, slightly wider mesh is better for boilies and pellets.

PVA mesh/stocking/web

This is one of the greatest inventions of modern carp fishing and has been directly responsible for the capture of many thousands of big carp. It's a strong filament that's loaded with bait, tied off at both ends to form a bag and then attached to the hook before it's cast out. Because PVA is water-soluble, when the bag of bait hits the bottom of the lake it quickly dissolves to release a neat payload of free offerings right next to the hookbait.

This accurate presentation of loosefeed, placed right next to the hookbait, adds a huge boost of attraction to draw carp to your hookbait and induce a bite.

Now for rigging up ...

You now have a guide to all the larger items of tackle you need, and how to set them up on the bank. We've also cut through the jungle of rig-making products to give you a simple list of the kit you need to make up the tackle that goes on the end of your mainline.

Over the next eight pages we'll show you how to tie a hooklink, how to set up two basic but very effective rigs and how you make use of PVA mesh.

Tying a hooklink

The short link between your mainline and the fish is the most important part of your whole carp-fishing set-up – get it right and you'll catch fish, get it wrong and you probably won't!

Ready-made hooklinks are available and they're good, but a far more economic way to fish is to tie your own hooklink, and that's what we're going to teach you here.

To show you two simple variations of hooklink, first we'll provide details of how to tie a link made from soft and supple braided line, then we'll show you how to use plastic-coated braid to produce a hybrid hooklink that's both stiff and supple.

Needless to say, these aren't the only hooklinks you can use to catch carp – there are many much more complicated set-ups that are claimed to have dramatic fish-catching properties; but carp fishing is only as complicated as you want to make it, and many carp anglers – newcomers and experienced fishermen alike – suffer from over complicating things.

The fact is that these two hooklinks will do the job in most fishing situations, and once you've mastered their use you'll find it easier to experiment with other set-ups when you're faced by especially tricky circumstances.

Let's start by looking at the braided rig.

Soft and supple – tying a braided hooklink

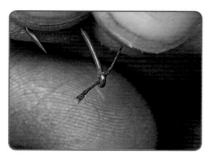

1 Braided lines are woven from man-made filaments to produce an exceptionally soft line that's very strong for its diameter. You also need a size 6–10 hook, a short silicone sleeve and a Korda Link Loop connector.

2 Cut off 18in (45cm) of braid – you'll need sharp scissors (called 'braid blades') to cut this tough line. In most circumstances a braid of around 12–18lb is a good choice.

3 Create a double overhand loop in one end of the braid. This will form the hair rig.

4 Thread the end of the braid through the rear of the hook eye.

5 Position the hair-rig loop below the bend of the hook – the distance will depend on the size of bait you use. There should be at least a centimetre gap between the bottom of the bend and the top of the bait when it's threaded on the hair loop.

6 Grab the line just above the hook and whip it round the shank just below the hook. Make sure the line is whipped down the side of the hook where there's no gap between the hook eye and the shank.

7 Whip down the shank 10 to 12 times until the whipping is almost level with the hookpoint.

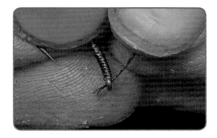

8 Thread the end of the hooklink back through the rear of the hook eye and pull it tight.

9 This whipping is known as the 'knotless knot'.

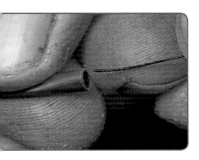

10 Slide the silicone sleeve down the hooklink. This will help stop tangles when you cast.

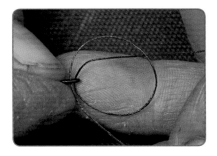

11 Thread the end of the line twice through a Korda Link Loop metal ring.

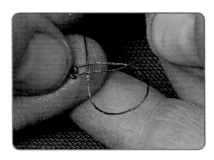

12 Position the ring 6–9in (15–23cm) from the hook, form a loop in the tag end of line and pass the tag end of braid through the loop.

13 Whip the tag end of line round the hooklink and the loop five times.

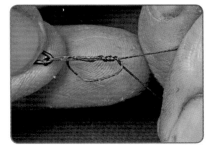

14 Before fully tightening the knot give it a slight pull to line it up like this.

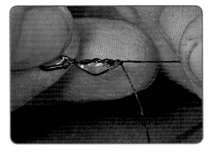

15 Moisten the twists of braid with saliva to lubricate it and help the line slide.

16 Smoothly pull the knot tight, easing it down to sit on the tip of the link loop. You've just tied a five-turn grinner knot.

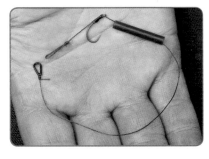

17 Here's the finished braided hooklink.

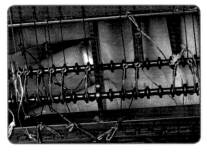

18 Store it on a rig board for ease of transport to the bank.

How to make a coated braid hooklink

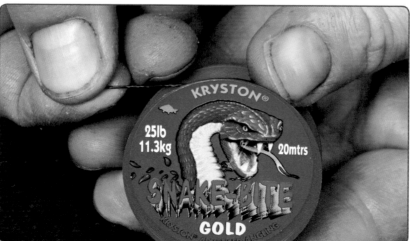

Coated braid offers one big advantage over uncoated braid – the plastic coating stiffens the line and makes it far less likely to tangle when casting. However, this stiffness does make the hookbait behave unnaturally when compared to the loose offerings fed into the swim. This is why you strip the coating near the hook to expose the soft braid core. Here's what you do…

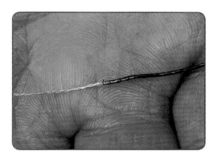

1 Before you tie the hair-rig loop, strip 10in (25cm) of coating off the coated braid with your fingernails.

2 This exposes the soft braided core that will end up near your hookbait to give it a more natural movement.

3 Tie the loop, thread the line through the rear of the hook eye and position the loop as in the braided hooklink sequence on the previous page.

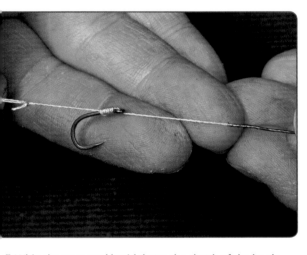

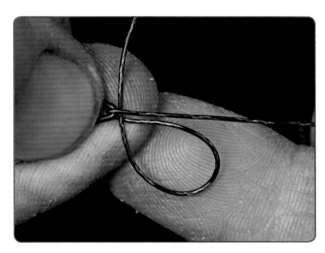

4 Whip the uncoated braid down the shank of the hook until the whipping is level with the hookpoint. Thread the end of the hooklink through the rear of the hook eye and pull tight.

5 Complete the link with a link loop in identical fashion to how the braided hooklink was tied.

6 Many coated braids will loop up off the bottom, which may spook wary carp. One or two small blobs of tungsten putty will pin it down.

7 The finished rig ready to be used. Pick a coated braid that matches the colour of the bottom in the lake you're going to fish – it will camouflage your rig.

Keep it simple

Now that you know how to tie a hooklink it's time to slot it on to the end of a rig.

Over the next four pages we'll show you how to tie two different rigs that suit most fishing situations. In extreme circumstances other rigs might be better but keeping it simple is usually one of the key skills to remember when specimen carp fishing. Many carp anglers needlessly complicate things when a simple rig is usually better.

Putting together a lead clip

There are many different brands of lead clip available but this system is one of the best and simplest to piece together. You can slot it together and be ready to fish in just a few minutes – who said carp fishing is complicated?

1 Here's what you need: a Korda Safezone Hybrid Lead Clip leader and the hooklink we showed you how to tie earlier.

2 Unravel the leader and pull it straight. It's stiffer than the mainline so it prevents tangles, and it's dotted with tungsten to pin it to the lake bed.

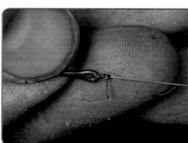

3 Use a five-turn grinner knot (see page 153) to attach the leader to the end of the mainline.

4 You need a hooklink clip to attach the hooklink to the swivel on the end of the leader.

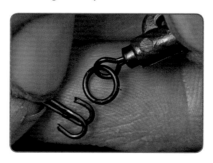

5 Pinch the clip to open it and slide it on to the swivel.

6 The hooklink clip sits on the swivel ready to accept the link loop on the end of the hooklink.

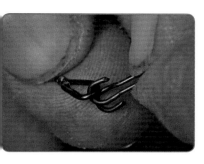

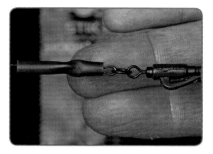

7 Pinch the clip to open it and slide the hooklink on to it.

8 The hooklink is now attached to the leader.

9 Slide the silicone sleeve on the hooklink over the clip and link loop. Leave the swivel free to spin.

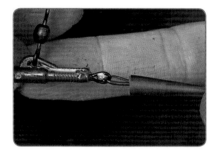

10 Fit the leger weight to the lead clip – the swivel of the leger should nestle in the recess of the clip.

11 Moisten the clip with saliva and slide the tail rubber on to it to secure the leger.

12 You don't need to push the tail rubber fully on to the lead clip.

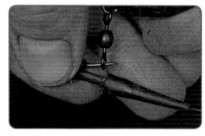

13 Ideally you want the clip to open out and release the leger if it gets snagged. It stops the rig tethering a fish if the line breaks and also makes it easier to land carp in weedy lakes.

14 Here's the finished rig ready to be baited and cast out.

15 This 48lb carp is my biggest fish caught in Britain and was landed on a lead clip rig.

Putting together a running leger clip

Tying a free-running rig is no more difficult than a lead clip thanks to the simple kits sold by many firms that are readily available in tackle shops. All of these kits share similar construction principles, so whichever package you pick the following guide will provide you with the step-by-step instruction you need to bolt together a great rig that will catch you lots of carp. Here's how you tie it…

1 There are lots of ready-made running leger kits available that make setting up these rigs very easy. This Korda kit is a very simple one to use.

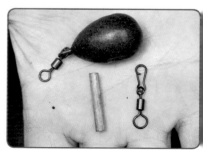

2 Start by making the sliding leger weight set-up. You need a 2–3oz lead, a piece of silicone sleeve and the swivel/clip arrangement supplied in the kit.

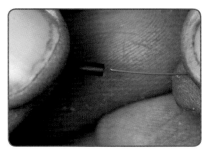

3 Attach the clip to the swivel, run the silicone sleeve on to a baiting needle and slide the sleeve over the clip.

4 Use pliers to cut the swivel off the leger and attach the brass loop to the clip. Slide the leger on to the anti-tangle tubing.

5 Thread the mainline into the hollow anti-tangle tubing. Cut the line at an angle with scissors to make it easier to thread.

6 Push the supplied buffer bead on to the end of the anti-tangle tubing and then tie the mainline emerging from the tubing to a swivel.

7 The swivel then pulls into the base of the bead and fixes.

8 Pinch the clip to open it and attach a hooklink.

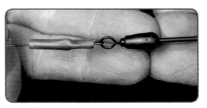

9 Cover the top of the hooklink and the clip with the silicone tubing sitting on the hooklink.

10 The finished set-up sees the leger sliding on the anti-tangle tubing. This is a very safe rig and allows you to carp-fish on venues where semi-fixed rigs (like the lead clip) are banned.

11 A 20lb-plus fish from Lemington Lakes. This fell to a running leger rig and gave a beautifully slow take as it pulled line through the sliding leger.

Boilies – cutting through the confusion

Boilies are purpose-made specialist carp bait that have been designed to resist the attention of small fish and select only the larger carp.

Made with a variety of powdered ingredients such as soya, semolina, milk protein, bird food and fishmeals, this base mix is made into a dough by adding eggs and liquid flavouring. This dough is rolled into balls and cooked (hence the name 'boilies') to make the baits go hard.

There are several key advantages that boilies provide the specialist carp angler:

- The hard texture resists interference from small fish such as roach, rudd and bream.
- Aerodynamically shaped, they catapult very well to help you bait up accurately.
- Loading boilies with flavours and enhancers creates a highly attractive bait.
- Hardening the bait means it can be left in the water a long time without disintegrating, and cast a long way without flying off the rig.
- Different ingredients can be used, enabling the angler to customise the smell, taste and attraction of their bait.
- Buoyant boilies can be made that lift (or 'pop up') off the lake bed to offer a hookbait variation.
- Boilies can be made to different sizes and shapes to provide you with an unusual bait that gives you a fishing 'edge'.

So, let's look at the main types of boilie you may need…

Left: This 20lb-plus carp fell to a frozen Nutrabaits Trigga Ice boilie.

DIY boilies

Bait companies make packaged base mixes of powdered ingredients and bottles of flavours and additives that can be added to blended eggs to form the boilie dough that's rolled into balls and cooked.

Rolling tables and sausage guns are available to allow you to roll your own perfectly round baits, which can be cooked and frozen for later use.

Ready-made boilies

This is the most popular type of boilie. Mixed, rolled, cooked and packaged by bait firms (above right), they're supplied in a mass of different sizes, colours and flavours.

Some are known as 'shelf-life' baits, as they've been specially preserved to stop them going mouldy. Others must be kept frozen until needed in order to keep them fresh.

Pop-up boilies

These baits (right) have been made with buoyant ingredients so that they can be popped up off the lake bed to offer the carp a very different form of presentation. This type of bait is especially useful when fishing in lakes where a carpet of weed coats the bottom, as it makes the hookbait stand out better and be easier for the fish to take.

Boilie additives

Whichever type of boilie you're using you can boost the bait by dosing it with potent bait soaks that are loaded with flavours and natural food extracts that scream 'food!' to a passing carp. Often known as 'glugs' (right), these liquids can be poured on to a boilie to enhance its attraction.

Hookbait options ...

Now we'll look at how these different boilies can be used to provide you with a highly attractive hookbait on the rigs we've already described.

As you'll see, one of the great things about using boilies is that you can produce a wide variety of different treats with which to tempt carp…

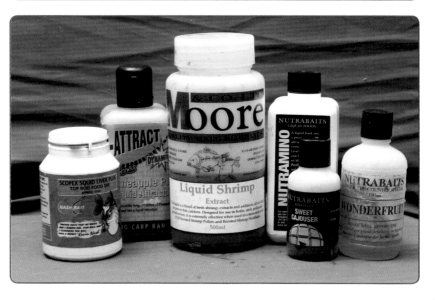

Hookbaits to catch carp

A basic boilie taken straight out of the bag and hair-rigged on a good rig does catch a lot of carp, but there are an awful lot of hookbait variations that can tempt their fair share of fish too.

Being creative and giving the fish something different to what they've become used to from lots of other anglers can give you an element of surprise that will stack the odds of a bite in your favour.

One of the most common additions to any hookbait is a flavour 'glug'. By soaking the boilie in liquid bait boosters you guarantee that a slick of attraction leaks out of the bait when it's been cast out and is lying on the lake bed. This can tempt fish into sampling your hookbait and may get you a bite when other anglers are struggling. Many bait companies produce purpose-made bait dips, soaks or glugs that will give a boilie a major lift. Many natural extracts are also worth a try.

Rather than soaking the bait directly in the concentrated flavouring, which is likely to be too strong, use one of these liquids in diluted form to boost your bait.

Here are some suggestions of ideas you could try…

The snowman
This presentation sees a normal sinking boilie joined on a longer hair rig by a second, buoyant (pop-up) bait (right). Looking like a snowman, the pop-up boilie counteracts the weight of the sinking bait and the hook to make it easier for a feeding fish to suck up the hookbait.

A variant of this rig sees the baits trimmed so that they only just sink to the bottom. Known as a critically balanced bait, this makes the hookbait a featherweight offering that will shoot into a carp's mouth when a minimum suck is aimed at it by a fish.

The pop-up
A buoyant pop-up boilie is threaded on to the hair rig, but to keep it pinned to the bottom a split shot is pinched to the line just below the hook. The positioning of this anchor shot dictates how far the hookbait will pop up off the lake bed – place the shot 2in (50mm) below the hook and the hookbait will pop up the same distance (below).

To present the pop-up the way you want it the shot must be tested in water before you cast out, to ensure that it's heavy enough to anchor the bait. The counterweight can be adjusted to critically balance the hookbait so that it's just heavy enough to pin it down.

Barrels and minis

The normal shape of a boilie is round, and they usually have a diameter of 14mm to 18mm. This can make the profile of a boilie very predictable in lakes that see a lot of baits fed into them, and carp may consequently regard them with some suspicion. In order to give them something different,

barrel-shaped boilies and mini baits of 8mm to 10mm (above) can be used instead.

Trim-downs and paste wraps

Another way to turn a round boilie into something less suspicious is to whittle away the edges to make it a different shape. Removing the skin like this has the secondary advantage of allowing the attractors locked inside the bait to leak into the water more easily.

Boosting the source of attraction like this is also the motivation behind wrapping a boilie in paste (below). With the hair-rigged boilie acting as an anchor the paste slowly dissolves to leak a slick of extra attractors into the water.

Peperami and fake tips

It might be an animal of a snack but Peperami sausage is also a great carp bait. Packed with garlic and spices, it's a very tasty bait that carp of all sizes love to eat at any time of year. To give it a boost you can cut away the skin to help it release its flavours more easily. You can also tip it with a piece of buoyant fake corn to give it a flash of colour and to negate the weight of the hook so that the bait shoots into a fish's mouth more easily.

Flavouring fakes

There are lots of fake baits available these days that look very similar to the real thing but which are made of plastic or rubber

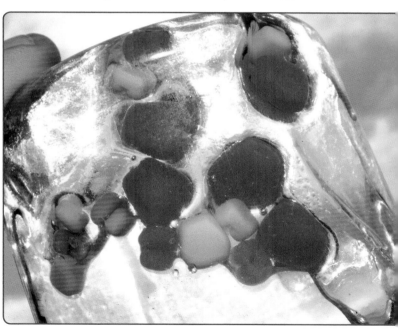

to render them more resistant to the attentions of small fish. Used on their own or added to another bait like a boilie, these fakes can be boosted by soaking them in flavouring.

The various sizes and colours of Enterprise Tackle fake corn in the picture have been soaked in Nashbaits sweetcorn extract – a sweet syrupy gunge that taints the dummy baits with a boost of attraction.

The PVA snack bag

Perhaps the easiest and most effective booster to your hookbait is the PVA snack bag, a small package of feed housed inside a water-soluble PVA mesh bag.

Attached to your hook prior to casting out, once the PVA bag hits the lake bed it soon melts and splits open, releasing its bait contents on to the bottom and attracting fish to the hookbait. It's a proven way to tempt more carp and here's how to do it…

1 Nutrabaits Trigga Ice freezer boilies – the author's favourite carp bait. Crush them against each other.

2 Load the resultant boilie crumb inside a PVA mesh tube system.

3 Add a few Trigga Ice pellets to the crumb.

4 Shake the contents into the bottom of the PVA mesh.

5 Tie the bag off tightly with an overhand knot and place it on the hook. Don't put the hook through the knot of PVA. Note the fake corn tipping the boilie hookbait.

6 Spear a piece of dissolving casting foam on the hookpoint and moisten the back of it to make it go sticky.

8 The finished rig ready for casting. The foam nugget helps to stop tangles and soon dissolves once the rig hits the lake bed to leave the hookbait lying alongside the patch of crumb and pellets falling from the bag.

7 Dampen a second foam nugget and stick it to the back of the other one to cover the hook. Pinch the corners to secure it.

9 A monster carp of 58lb that fell for the PVA rig.

Spot-on casting

Casting accurately and consistently is one of the keys to catching carp. They're fish that frequent the same places to feed, meaning that it's often essential that you can cast on to exactly the right spot – missing by a few feet can make a big difference.

There are also occasions when carp show on the surface at long range, so you've also got to be able to cast far enough to reach them but still retain the accuracy of your casting.

In this picture sequence we'll show you the essential steps you must take to ensure that your rig finds the mark time after time – which will help you catch more fish.

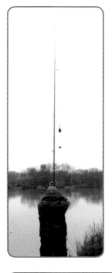

1 Wind up your rig until it's hanging 4–5ft (1.2–1.5m) down from the tip. Leaving a long drop like this helps you compress the rod during casting, which gets you extra distance on the cast. Line up the rod with the spot you want to target.

2 The rod is in line with your nose so it's smack between your eyes. With the bail arm on the reel open and the line hooked around your finger, drop the rig behind you so that it's in the ten o'clock position.

3 Swing the rig backwards slightly, then sweep it forward to propel the leger at its target. Release the line as the rod hits the two o'clock position.

4 As the lead flies through the air point the rod in the two o'clock position, with your finger over the spool lip ready to dab the line pouring off the spool just before the rig hits the water. This is called 'feathering the line' and helps avoid tangles. It also allows you to cut the flight of the leger and drop it where you want it to land.

5 When you've landed the rig in the right spot tighten the line and slip it into the clip on the side of the spool. This limits the distance of re-casts and ensures that they land in the same spot every time you cast.

6 With the mainline in the clip pull it tight to the leger and tie on a marker knot of No 3 pole elastic a few inches beyond the rod tip. To recast accurately wind the knot to the same position and clip up the line near the reel – this way you know your casting distance is limited to the same range every time.

7 When casting to the clip launch out the rig and just before it hits the water pull the rod vertically in the air like this. As the line pulls tight to the clip follow the leger with the rod to cushion it and drop the rig in the water where you want it.

8 This 24lb mirror carp took a hookbait that was cast with the help of a line clip and a marker knot to land it 'on the money' in a clear area amid thick weed. To find this spot a marker float was essential, so let's look at how you use one…

Mapping your swim – how to use a marker float

The ability to read what's under the surface of the water is a vital carp-fishing skill.

The surface of a lake gives little or no indication as to what's going on below the waterline, and there isn't a single lake that's entirely uniform in depth, has an unchanging make-up of lake bed, or lacks some variation in topography that can influence fish behaviour and feeding patterns.

In some lakes the underwater features you're looking for are subtle – maybe a marginal drop-off where the depth increases by a foot – but in other pools the changes are massive.

In former gravel pits that only came into existence as a result of quarrying, the fingerprint of man is all over the carp's underwater habitat. Deep trenches, steep bars or large shallow plateaux can be scattered across such venues. To carp these features act like roadways or navigation points as they roam around the fishery looking for food, and in many instances the carp will frequent certain areas because the features that are found there actually encourage the creation of a natural food larder.

For example, at the bottom of a steep gravel bar there's often a pocket of silt and food. Find a bed of sunken weed and you've found something that harbours water snails and shrimp. If you locate a soft patch of silt surrounded by hard clay or gravel you've found a breeding ground for bloodworm – one of a carp's staple food sources. If you can find these feeding areas and place your baits nearby the chances of you catching are greatly increased.

There are areas in most lakes that you could probably fish forever without catching a carp, but there are also spots that are 'bankers' for action. If you can find and avoid the barren areas and concentrate your attack on the productive feeding spots you'll catch more carp.

It's strange, then, that for such a vital fish-finding skill that can have such a major bearing on what they catch, so many carp anglers pay so little attention to mapping out the lake bed.

Feature-finding with a marker float set-up does take time but it's never wasted. It might be a cliché, but having a hookbait in the right spot for an hour is better than having a bait in the wrong spot for a day.

The picture sequence below shows a simple marker float set-up and how it works. If you're serious about your carp fishing it's *essential* that you take time out to map the lake bed of your fishery in this way. Over a period of time you'll piece together a more detailed understanding of your lake and you'll see your results get better and better. Here's how you do it…

1 **This is a classic marker float set-up that works well. Sold as a complete kit by Korda, the buoyant stem that runs on the braided mainline features a large ring on the end to allow the line** to slide through it easily. The buoyancy of the stem itself is designed to lift the line above any weed on the bottom to allow the depth to be measured properly. On the end of the line is a large vaned float that's visible at long range and is buoyant enough to pull the line through the stem and rise to the surface.

2 **This diagram shows you how the float works. It's cast out and the float is tightened down to the leger; then you let out a foot (30cm) of line at a time until the float reaches the surface. This allows you to record the depth of the water, and repeated casting around the swim will allow you to piece together a map of the lake bed and any depth changes.

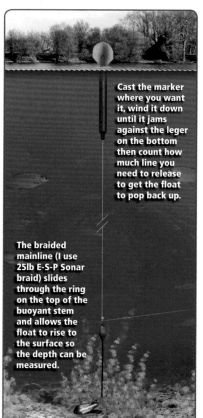

Cast the marker where you want it, wind it down until it jams against the leger on the bottom then count how much line you need to release to get the float to pop back up.

The braided mainline (I use 25lb E-S-P Sonar braid) slides through the ring on the top of the buoyant stem and allows the float to rise to the surface so the depth can be measured.

3 **One of the most essential pieces of tackle for marker-float work is 25 to 35lb braided mainline. The lack of stretch and the low diameter of the braid not only helps you cast the float further but i also helps you measure the depth more accurately, and, most importantly, feel th difference in the make-up of the lake bed**

As you pull the leger across the bottom on braid you'll feel every bump and movement as the braid sends vibrations shooting up the line and into the rod. You'll soon learn that a smooth slide means the lead is on sand, you'll recognise the solid plug and release of the lead landing in silt, and you'll also learn to feel the leger snagging and tearing through heavy weed growth.

4 To use the marker float set-up, cast out to the area you want to map and then wind the reel line in until you feel the float tighten down to the leger on the bottom. Now slacken the drag system on the reel so that the braid can be pulled off the spool easily.

5 Pull braid off the reel a foot (30cm) at a time. You'll see the slack in the line immediately get taken up as the float starts its rise to the surface. Make sure you count the number of times you release line.

6 Many custom-made marker rods have markings on them to register the amount of line being released to the float. If your rod doesn't have this feature you need to measure and mark these distances on the blank so that you can measure depth accurately.

7 By repeatedly pulling off line and counting the accumulation of braid being let out you'll be able to gauge the depth and mark any changes. Write down these measurements so that you can create your own swim-by-swim map of your lake.

8 When the flight of the float appears it indicates that the line between the leger on the bottom and the float is straight and allows you to get an accurate picture of what depth the water really is.

9 In this picture the float is marking the point where a slope reaching out from the island levels off – there's no clue about this by simply looking at the surface of the lake. Only a marker float will allow you to find such potentially significant features.

10 In addition to allowing you to map a swim a marker float can also be used as a baiting target, especially when you're casting into open water where there are no visible features to act as rangefinders. Catapulting your loosefeed around the float allows you to create a baited area near the feature you've pinpointed. Your baited rigs can also be cast to the float and the line distance marked on them so that any re-casts will land in the right spot.

11 When using a marker float to feel the make-up of the lake bed the float is wound down to the leger to pull the braided line tight. Point the rod directly at the leger then slowly sweep the rod through a 90° arc, dragging the lead across the bottom. The lack of stretch in the braid means that any change in the nature of the lake bed will echo up the line and straight into your hands. You'll soon learn to read these signs and map out differences in the lake bed.

12 Here's a nice carp that was landed thanks to a spot of detailed feature-finding. It was caught from a small gravel patch surrounded by thick weed. As carp often clear an area they regularly feed in, finding this feature indicated a probable feeding spot. It also allowed me to present the hookbait cleanly without burying it in heavy weed.

Spodding – the accurate way to bait up

Baiting up your carp swim accurately is a key aspect to consistently catching carp – to put it bluntly, one of the things that sets the most successful carpers apart from the less successful ones is the way they apply loosefeed and how accurate they are with their baiting operations.

While carp will readily eat large food items such as 14mm or 18mm boilies which can usually be catapulted to the area you want to target, a more natural feeding situation is to use smaller baits like pellets, hempseed or even small boilies that could never be catapulted to the range you want to fish. You must remember that carp are naturally programmed to eat bloodworm, water snails, shrimp and other tiny bugs and grubs. If you can create a baited area that mimics this natural feeding situation you stand to regularly catch large fish.

This is why the bait rocket – otherwise known as a 'spod' – has become one of the key weapons in the carp anglers' armoury.

Put simply, a spod is a hollow, aerodynamic plastic tube with a nosecone that's made from extremely buoyant material that will cause the spod to turn upside down when it hits the water. The tube is loaded with bait, cast to the spot you want to fish, and the nosecone does the rest of the job for you – it upends the spod and dumps the contents where you want them. There's no better way to create a neatly baited area that simply can't be created with a catapult.

Spodding is a specialist feeding technique, though, and it requires you to buy purpose-made tackle because a loaded spod is likely to weigh 4–5oz (115–140g), which places huge strain on your kit when you cast. Consequently the tackle you use must be stepped up to cope with the pressure.

Many companies now make spodding rods, usually a 12ft beefcake with a test curve of 3.5lb to 4.5lb. As with the marker-float work already detailed, it pays to use 20lb low-diameter braided mainline such as Berkley Fireline or Whiplash and a shockleader of Korda's 30lb or 50lb Arma-Kord – a super-tough braid that can take the strain of repeated spodding.

Here's a simple guide to spodding that will get you baiting accurately and effectively…

1 Here's a typical spod, a hollow plastic tube that's loaded with bait before being cast to the spot you've marker-floated and picked as your target area. The bright nosecone flips the spod upside down to release the bait and acts as a 'sight bob' to tell you when the rocket has turned over and dropped its payload. This is the cue to re-cast.

2 There are different sizes of spods available. Obviously the bigger the spod the more bait it will carry and the faster it will introduce the bait you want to feed, but this will also make it weigh a lot more. If you're a newcomer to spodding you'll almost certainly find it easier to spod with a smaller, lighter spod; they're easier to cast accurately and any 'dud' casts you make won't introduce too much bait where you don't want it.

3 A modern Dyneema superline like Berkley Whiplash aids your spodding massively. The lack of stretch allows all the power of the cast to be directed into launching the spod, while the low diameter of the line ensures that the spod flies straight and reaches maximum range. If you use a marker float to pinpoint the area you want to feed, cast your spod there and clip up the line to ensure each cast hits the spot

4 This is the junction between the low-diameter mainline braid and the tougher Arma-Kord shockleader material – directions for tying this knot are supplied with the Arma-Kord. Notice how much thicker the shockleader braid is. This ensures that it withstands the strain of repeated spodding.

5 Before casting a spod, guide the knot down to the rear of the reel spool. This ensures that the line doesn't repeatedly rub over the knot on the cast which will reduce your casting performance and may cause tangles.

6 Ensure there are six to eight wraps of shockleader around the reel when the spod is in position for casting. Leave a long drop of 5–6ft (1.5–1.8m) between spod and rod tip when you cast – this aids smooth casting and helps you compress the stiff spodding rod to generate casting power.

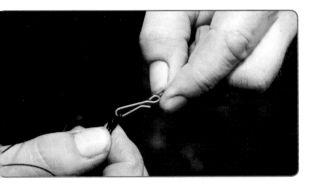

7 The spod should be attached to the shockleader with a heavy-duty sea-fishing clip. This is tough enough to withstand casting and allows you to quickly clip and unclip a spod.

8 Small baits such as hemp and 4–6mm pellets are ideal for loading inside a spod. They're great baits that carp love to eat and they can't be fed at range with a catapult because they're too lightweight.

9 Don't overfill a spod. They cast best if you leave a fifth or a quarter of the spod empty when casting.

10 Small boilies can also be packed inside a spod. Again, don't overfill the spod or you'll spill a lot of feed on the cast and unbalance the spod.

11 Once the spod is loaded, the shockleader correctly sited on the reel and the mainline clipped up at the range you want to hit, line up the cast.

12 Launch the spod with a slightly slower action than you would when casting a lighter leger – a smooth and sweeping casting motion will fire out the loaded rocket.

13 If you've cast accurately at the marker float the line clip on the reel will check the distance of the cast and bring it splashing down alongside the float.

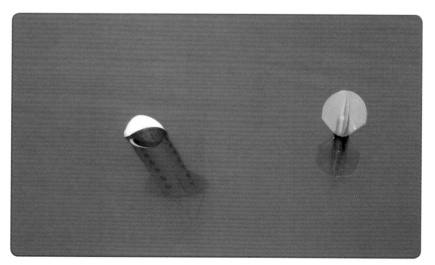

14 The nosecone flips the spod upside down and the loosefeed tumbles out, creating a bed of bait around the float. How much you feed depends on the quantity of carp and how well they're feeding. Just remember that it's easy to quickly put in a lot of bait with a spod and that you can easily *overbait* the swim and make your hookbait appear like the proverbial needle in a haystack. Four or five spod-loads is often a good starting point unless you're confident the carp are feeding strongly.

15 This 41lb common carp fell to a baited area that was laced with 10mm boilies, small pellets and bits of crushed boilie. Baits like this can't be catapulted very far, but an accomplished spodder can cast them 100yd (90m) or more.

Landing, unhooking, weighing and releasing a carp

When your rig, bait and location all slot into place it's only a matter of time until your bite alarm calls you into action – now the fun begins!

One of the things that most impresses newcomers to carp fishing is the fight in these fish. They really are the musclemen of the underwater world and they often battle like their very lives depend on escape. So what happens when you do hook one? How do you cope with the speed and power of their initial run? How do you avoid losing the fish during an extended battle?

The answer is in the sequence of photographs below; but the key element you must remember is *patience*. The fact is that as long as you've chosen the right breaking strain of line and tough enough hooks you really should lose very few carp as long as you don't get a rush of blood to the head and try to rush the fish into the net. If you try and bundle a carp into the net before it's ready the ratio of lost fish to landed fish will go very much in the favour of the carp.

So, here's a guide to playing and landing a carp, plus details of what you do to ensure the fish you catch go back to the water none the worse for their exertions. Carp are big and powerful fish but they're also quite delicate once they're out of the water, and they need to be looked after. Here's how you do it.

1 As a fish picks up your hookbait and pulls the hook home against the weight of the semi-fixed leger weight, it will bolt away from the resistance and your bite alarm will light up as line is pulled from the reel.

2 To ensure that this initial rush doesn't prove disastrous your drag or freespool mechanism must be adjusted so that line is released from the spool long before the breaking strain is reached. Adjust the tension while pulling line off the reel to get the right resistance.

3 When the fish is running don't 'strike' into the bite as you would if you were float fishing and had to connect with a lightning-quick roach bite. The leger has already hooked the carp for you – just pick up the rod and tighten the line to secure the hookhold.

4 If you've adjusted the drag-setting properly a fast-running fish will be able to pull line off the reel smoothly. Some anglers prefer to disengage the anti-reverse – this allows the reel handle to be rotated backwards to release more line to the hooked fish. However, although this releases line it doesn't give you as much control as using a quality drag system.

5 Once the carp's initial rush has been curbed, start to pump the fish back towards the bank. To do this lower the rod while winding in the slack line, then ease it back to the vertical position. Always keep the rod bent and the line tensioned. The carp may rush off again at any time so don't tighten the drag up just in case – if the carp wants to run, let it.

6 Once you've patiently played much of the carp's fight out of it ease it higher in the water and draw it towards the bank. Ease the landing net into the water by your feet and sink the mesh. Slowly ease the fish to the surface and towards the waiting net.

7 Lay the rod back on the rests and pull the net into the margins.

8 Brace your forearm across the two arms of the net and prize them out of the landing net spreader block.

9 Gather the mesh to create a cradle for the fish to lie in. Make sure all its fins are lying flat to its body and then lift it out of the water.

10 Carry the fish over to the unhooking mat, which should be positioned close behind your rod set-up. The weigh sling should already be laid in the base of the mat.

11 There are many different types of mat available, many of which are thick, cushion-style mats packed with foam or polystyrene beads – they do a good job. However, my favourite is this hammock-style design that holds the fish off the ground; this is a Nash Carp Cradle.

12 Use a set of forceps to ease the hook out of the fish. Don't yank the hook, just clamp the forceps on and rotate your wrist to tease the hook out.

13 You can also dab the hooking point with medicated carp-care liquid.

14 Slide the net out from under the fish. This allows the carp to be transferred to the weigh sling without being lifted.

15 Gather the sling and secure the sides to stop the carp sliding out as you lift it. The soaked sling should be put on the scales before the fish is brought to the mat and either zeroed or the weight noted so that it can be deducted later to get an accurate weight.

16 Place the sling on the scales and weigh the carp. Keep a firm grip on the scales in case the fish flaps in the sling, and hold the scales at the top to get an accurate weight.

17 If you want a photograph of yourself with the fish lower it back down on to the mat and open the sling again. Douse it with water to keep it wet and healthy.

18 Slide one hand round the wrist of the carp's tail and put the other hand around the pectoral fins under the fish's gill plate. Grip the fish firmly – you won't hurt it and it's less likely to slip or jump out of your hands. Hold the fish over the mat and hold it close to your body so that you have control of it.

19 When the photo has been taken lower the carp back into the sling, secure the sides and carry it to the water.

20 Hold the fish in the water for a moment until it's breathing well and kicking its tail. Then pull the sling apart and allow the fish to slide out and into the water before it swims away. You've landed, weighed, photographed and released the fish with minimum disturbance to the carp.

PIKE FISHING

Understanding pike fishing   176

Essential kit for piking   178

Tying a wire trace   181

Setting up a float rig   186

Mounting deadbaits and a long-range leger rig   188

Looking after your pike   190

Understanding pike fishing

Pike are the sharks of the freshwater world. Lean, mean, armed with a fearsome array of weaponry and utterly ruthless, these supreme predators are a roach's worst nightmare and their razor-sharp teeth are the very last thing that many small fish will ever see.

Fishing for pike is necessarily a specialist occupation. Not only does their potential size require you to step up your gear, but the deadly set of teeth they possess also means you must use super-tough wire hooklinks and hooks that could slam the anchors on a supertanker.

If you don't gear up properly for pike fishing you WILL come off second best.

While there's a huge range of different tactics to catch pike, in this guide we're going to concentrate on the two most basic methods that will suit the vast majority of fishing situations on most venues – float-fished deadbaits and legered deadbaits.

But before we look at these tactics in detail we first need to understand this unusual species. If you don't know what makes these predators tick you'll find it far harder to catch them.

Meet the pike

Compared to the majority of freshwater species that have a great many characteristics in common, the pike is something of a loner both in terms of behaviour and physique.

Unlike non-predatory species that tend to group together into shoals, pike are solitary hunters that only come into close proximity with other pike at spawning time and in areas where an accumulation of food fish has a magnetic appeal to predators.

The most obvious sign that these fish are killers is the rows of razor-sharp teeth that line their mouth. In the lower jaw you'll find a chain of triangular-shaped fangs that are designed to puncture and fatally disable food fish. Frighteningly sharp and coated with an anti-coagulant that stops a wounded fish stemming a flow of blood from a bite, these are the teeth that usually bring down the curtain on a silverfish's life.

The angler too must treat these teeth with respect. They're incredibly sharp and can cause nasty injuries if you don't learn how to unhook your pike carefully and methodically, a skill that's described on page 190.

In the roof of the pike's mouth you'll find another gruesome-looking mass of teeth. Totalling several hundred individual gnashers, these smaller teeth are made to grip, turn and aid the

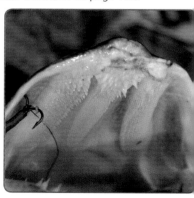

wallowing of prey fish. Packed into dense pads, each ne of these needle-sharp teeth points slightly backwards, a esign that helps to grip a captured fish and guide it down the ke's throat, since pike swallow their prey whole before they st up to digest their meal. This characteristic explains much f the pike's feeding behaviour, as they tend to be binge-aters that look to have a big meal and then lay dormant.

At times this means pike can be difficult to tempt – if it's tting on a full belly it may be hard to entice a pike into aving another meal. But the other side of this coin is that hen a pike is hungry it will stop at nothing to satisfy its unger, and they can be incredibly easy to catch when ney're gripped by bloodlust.

But like most top predators the most obvious sign of their unting ability shouldn't disguise a more sophisticated rmoury. For a start the pike has huge forward-pointing eyes nat are positioned at the end of two deep 'target' grooves ning the snout. These give the pike fabulous eyesight and n ability to judge distance. This gives them a major dvantage over prey fish – the pike can see them whereas ne prey may not see the pike – but it also explains why pike ften home in quickly on an angler's deadbait.

Pike that are on the lookout for a meal will instantly spot bait cast near them and will often race to grab a deadbait nat has only just sunk. For this reason it often pays to re-cast egularly when deadbaiting for pike – if the fishing is poor st winding in your bait and re-casting can spark an attack.

Pike also have an acute sense of smell, thanks to the large ostrils located on the front of their heads that help them ack down potential meals. This explains why potent-

smelling sea fish such as mackerel and sardines make such good hookbaits.

But something that really sets the pike apart is its ability to locate prey by vibration – located along the underside of its jaw and ringing the front of its head are a set of pits (pictured above and bottom left) that are loaded with sensors capable of picking up the movements of potential prey, especially injured fish that are moving erratically. These sensors also pick up the splashdown of a deadbait or the twitches of a livebait.

With their lean powerful muscles designed to make blisteringly quick sprints, the pike is a perfectly honed hunter that can snare its victim in the blink of an eye.

Deadly but delicate

Though pike look fearsome you shouldn't make the mistake of thinking they're tough – these are delicate fish that must be treated with the utmost care to ensure they're returned safely to the water once captured.

Later in this chapter we look at fish care, and this is a critical skill to master. Before anyone goes fishing for pike they must have the appropriate equipment and technique to look after these magnificent but ultimately fragile fish. It's also important that you use tackle that can cope with the deadly teeth lining its mouth, and no matter what rig you're using it's essential that you learn how to tie a wire trace. In this chapter top pike angler Mick Rouse (below) will show you how it's all done.

Essential kit for piking

Pike are a fish you don't mess about with when it comes to the essential kit you need to catch them. For starters the tackle must be able to withstand their teeth, which will mince kit that's not up to the job; it has also got to cope with the power of the fish, the blistering turn of speed they possess and the strain of casting out a large deadbait which might weigh several ounces.

All told this means that your tackle has got to be strong and durable. There's really no getting away from the fact that you've got to gear yourself up properly for pike fishing because if you try to skimp on things or just reuse kit you use for other types of fishing you're almost certainly heading for disaster.

Before we delve into the detail of rigs, baits and a host of pike-fishing tactics, here's a run-down of the gear you need.

Pick a strong rod

This is a basic step but an obvious one. You simply can't cast a deadbait any sort of distance unless you use a powerful 12ft-long rod that's a test curve of between 2.75lb and 3.5lb for extreme range fishing. As a rule a 3lb rating is about right for most anglers and if cash is tight you can get away with using a carp rod of the same test curve if you already have one.

However, most major manufacturers produce purpose-made pike rods that have slightly different characteristics to a carp rod. They tend to have a stiffer action, especially in the butt section, to help with casting heavy deadbaits and

the rod rings are also beefed up. Basically pike rods are more robust and pokier than carp rods and if you intend to go piking regularly it is worth investing in rods for the job.

Has your reel got the guts?

Pike fishing requires the use of thick, strong reel lines and in some cases you may be looking to cast 50, 60 or 70yd – this means you've got to use a large capacity reel. A 6, 8 or 10,000-size reel is what you need; go any smaller and you'll find that the heavy line pulling off the front lip of the spool will hinder your casting performance, and the distance you can push your rig will be reduced.

Load the reel with a minimum of 15lb monofilament or heavy-duty sinking braid of 30lb-plus, as you need to be sure that your line is strong enough to cope with the strain of repeatedly casting a baited rig, won't be snapped by a big fish and won't be easily broken if a hooked fish ploughs into reeds or weed.

Also remember to check your mainline regularly for damage, strip away any frayed line immediately and retie to fresh undamaged mono or braid.

This Daiwa Linear reel (above) is a good choice, not just because they're big and strong but because they have a precise front drag system that helps with playing fish and a freespool facility that can be slackened off to allow a pike that picks up and runs with the bait to pull line off the reel easily. Unlike some freespool systems this reel releases line with a clearly audible 'click', so if you happen to turn your eyes from a float for a second the reel may alert you to a particularly savage pick-up on the float rig that we'll detail later. This doesn't mean that you can ignore the float, because it's essential you watch it and strike a bite quickly when a pike grabs it; but if you've had your attention distracted the freespool system is an extra warning system and stops a pike pulling your rod into the water.

Have you got big arms?

Pike are long fish so you can't get away with using a net any smaller than one with 36in arms, and a 42in net is better. If you do hook a big pike – unknown giants turn up in unexpected places every year – you'd kick yourself

forever if you lost the fish of a lifetime because you were trying to fit it in a net that was too small!

Tough stuff

When it comes to tying your end tackle you need to gear up for pike carefully. As we'll detail later you can't use a hooklink made with nylon monofilament or braid, nor can you use normal strength hooks. A pike's jaw is lined with rows of teeth that will make short work of weak kit like this. Instead you've got to make hooklinks (called 'traces' when pike fishing) out of 30lb-plus wire and you've got to use strong size 4 or 6 treble hooks (below) to hold the bait and hook the fish.

Care for your catch

Just as important as using kit that can't be smashed up by a pike is taking care of your catch to ensure that it goes back in the water safely to live long and grow even bigger. This means that a thick, padded unhooking mat to lay the fish on is essential, as are pliers, forceps and cutters with which you'll remove the hooks quickly and safely – a skill we'll cover later in the chapter.

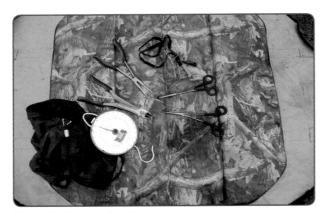

Above: Dedicated unhooking gear is essential.

Pike might be big and have a deadly set of teeth but they're not very robust and you must look after the fish you catch.

Oooops!

It's going to happen, so accept it and plan for it happening: no matter how careful you are, if you catch plenty of pike then sooner or later you'll get a little too close to those sharp teeth or a set of treble hooks! So always carry a small first aid kit with antiseptic dressings and waterproof plasters so that you can seal any small cuts and stop infection.

Extras

Pike fishing is a strong-arm branch of fishing that makes use of big baits and powerful tackle. This means you'll need to use large floats and other specialist bits of pike kit such as drop-off bite indicators, which we'll show you later.

However, don't let unusual items of kit like this put you off trying to catch a pike – compared to most types of fishing it's relatively easy to get into and you won't need too many specialist items, nor will you need to rob a bank to pay for a mountain of new kit. Pike fishing is an essentially simple pursuit.

Deadbaits

Finally there's the bait itself, and in this introduction to pike fishing we're only dealing with deadbaits, as they're most readily available and are proven fish catchers. Deadbaiting is also allowed on more venues than livebaits, so it makes sense to cover the use of dead fish as pike bait.

While almost any fish could theoretically be used to catch pike, deadbaits fall into two categories: sea fish and freshwater species.

The main sea fish that are used to catch pike are mackerel (below), smelt, herring, pollan and sprats. These are all oily and pungent fish with proven track records for attracting pike.

As for freshwater fish baits, the most obvious are deadbaits of typical prey fish such as roach, skimmer bream, rudd, trout, eel section and perch.

In recent years a number of unusual baits have also gained greater popularity, most notably the lamprey. This eel-like fish is filled with bloody juices that pike adore, and it has gained a great reputation as being one of the most reliable of pike baits.

Let's look at how you use kit like this to catch pike…

Tying a wire trace

sing a wire hooklink or trace is an absolute essential when
ke fishing. Tackling up with a strong monofilament
hooklength is totally unacceptable, as the pike's lethal teeth
an slice thick nylon like a hot knife through butter, and this
an leave a pike carrying treble hooks in its mouth.

In the following sequence Mick Rouse shows you how to
e a simple but reliable wire trace that's tough enough to
rithstand a pike's teeth. This trace can be used with either
f the two rigs we're going to show you in this chapter.

It's worth sounding one note of warning though. No
atter how good a wire trace is, it can be damaged by poor
knotting or a particularly vicious fight from a hooked pike.
Consequently you should check the trace every time you
wind in to re-cast or land a fish, and immediately change a
link that's kinked or frayed.

It's also essential that you follow Mick's advice to the
letter – shortening the trace, for example, can result in a
bite-off as pike can suck in the bait so far that its teeth close
around the nylon mainline and slice through it.

But if you buy the right kit and follow this simple step-by-
step guide you'll soon be tying quality wire traces that will
do the job perfectly.

1 Here's a list of the kit you need to tie a wire trace:

- **A set of quality heavy-duty scissors.** Mick has used this Kitchen Devil pair for five years, and repeatedly cutting wire still hasn't blunted them.
- **Fox Predator Easy Twist wire.** Use a minimum of 30lb breaking strain. It should be emphasised here that the technique used in this sequence won't work for stiff wire or coated wire – you must use twisting wire, which is actually easier to handle as it's pliable and doesn't kink easily.
- **Size 4 to 6 semi-barbed treble hooks.** These 2XS Fox trebles are strong and have one barbed hook (for lodging in the deadbait) and two barbless hooks that are easier to remove from a pike. Size 4 hooks are used for large deadbaits while 6s are best for the majority of most normal-sized deadbaits. Don't skimp on hooks, they take a lot of strain.
- **Fox Size 7 Cross Eye Power Swivels.** These strong swivels have one round eye on to which the nylon mainline is knotted and a diamond eye that's ideal for the wire to be attached.
- **Twiddling stick.** A useful little tool that helps massively when you're tying wire traces.
- **Greys Prowla Treble sleeves.** Not essential, but ideal for neatening wire knots. The red colour is chosen for two reasons: firstly it's an advert to an eagle-eyed pike, and secondly it allows the angler to instantly see where the hooks are when it comes to unhooking a fish.
- **Greys Prowla large Crimp Covers.** They push over the end of the swivel to cover the sharp tag end of the wire knot and reduce the chance of tangles on the cast.

2 Pull off 24in (60cm) of 30lb Easy Twist wire. Long traces are safer for the fish, and the finished trace should be 20in (50cm) long.

3 Cut the wire.

4 The treble that goes on the end of the hooklink is tied on first. Double-back the end of the wire to create a 2in (5cm) loop.

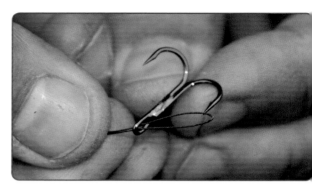

5 Nip the wire with your fingertip to flatten the loop and pass it through the eye of the hook.

6 Pass the loop over all three of the hook points.

7 Position the loop against the hooklink wire and start to pull it tight.

8 Slide the loop down the hooklink towards the hook eye.

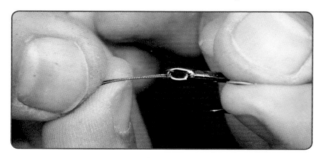

9 Pull both ends of the wire away from the hook to tighten the loop around the eye. Do NOT allow the wire to slip over the eye and sit around the hook shank.

10 Place the twiddling stick in the eye of the hook if it fits, or in the bend of one of the hooks. Use your thumb to place the tag end at a right angle.

11 While holding the trace tight, twiddle the stick to twist the tag end around the trace wire. Use your finger and thumb to apply pressure while twisting. Do 12–15 turns of wire to prevent any slippage.

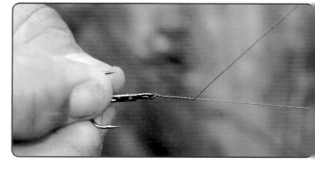

12 This is the neatly knotted bottom hook gripped by the wire – it'll never slip.

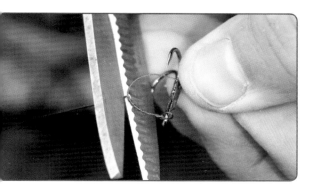

13 Cut off the tag end as close as possible.

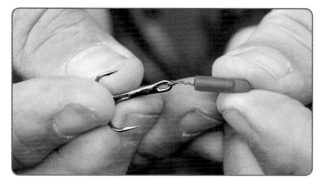

14 Slide the treble sleeve on to the wire and down to the hook.

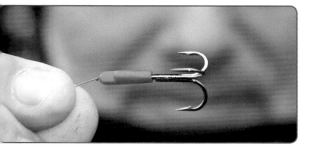

15 The finished hook, knotted and sleeved off.

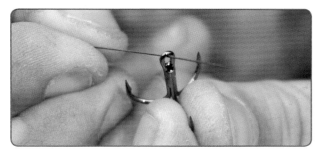

16 Now thread the wire through the eye of the top treble hook.

17 Measure the distance between the two hooks. For small baits such as smelt, sardines and lamprey section use size baits set 4in (10cm) apart.

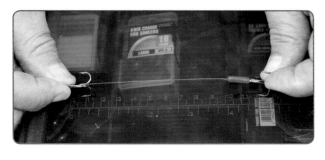

18 For bigger baits such as half mackerel, herring and large coarse baits use size 4 hooks set 5in (13cm) apart.

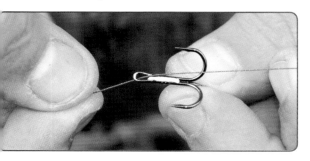

19 Lay the trace down the shank of the top hook with the bottom treble dangling below it. Hold the tag end of the wire above the hook eye.

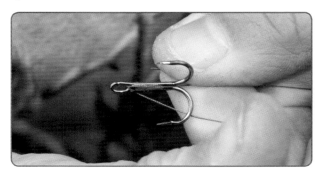

20 Loop the tag end of the trace back on itself along the shank and behind one of the treble hooks.

21 Pull the wire tight into the junction between the three hooks.

22 Whip five tight turns of wire up the shank towards the hook eye.

23 Thread the tag end back through the eye of the hook.

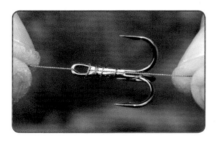

24 Pull the wire tight to fix the hook position.

25 Cover the upper treble with another hook sleeve.

26 Slide the large Prowla crimp sleeve on to the wire trace.

27 Here's the special cross-eye swivel – the round end is knotted to the monofilament mainline while the trace wire is fixed to the diamond-shaped eye.

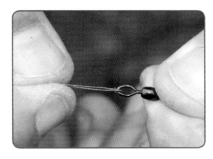

28 Double-back the wire to form a loop and pass it through the ...amond eye.

29 Pass the loop of wire over the round eye of the swivel.

30 Pull the loop tight to the top of the swivel.

31 Put the twiddling stick in the diamond eye and twist it 12 ...mes to fix the wire to the swivel.

32 Cover the twisted knot with the crimp sleeve.

33 One 20in (50cm) wire trace ready to be loaded on to a rig bin for later use.

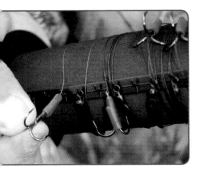

34 Rig bins like this are ideal for storing wire traces. The swivel ...fixed to the anchor point, the wire is ...rapped around the bin and the hooks ...re sunk into the soft rubber. This trace ...an now be fished on a float rig.

Setting up a float rig

Now that you've tied a wire trace you need to load it on to a rig that allows you to cast out a bait and spot a bite from a pike.

This rig is a hybrid presentation that allies a large pencil float for bite indication with an anchor leger that aids casting and holds the bait in place. Obviously the float is there to indicate a bite, so keep your eyes locked on it and strike as soon as it shows significant movement. In some cases the float will go under, on other occasions it'll drag across the surface, and sometimes it will suddenly rise or even lay flat on the surface if a pike picks up the bait and lifts the anchor weight off the bottom. Whatever type of indication you get you need to strike quickly to avoid deep-hooking the pike.

Very few components are required to tie the rig, and it doesn't need any special skills to make this simple and versatile set-up. It's a rig that experienced pike angler Mick Rouse uses for most of his fishing on lakes and slow-moving waterways. Here's how you bolt it together...

1 This is the kit you need to tie this float rig:

- **Fox Braid Stops. These rubber stops are designed to be slid on to the 15lb mainline and grip it firmly – this allows you to set the depth of the float rig.**
- **A large Fox Deadbait Pencil float. These huge balsa floats give great visibility over long distances and superb bite registration.**
- **Greys Prowla Quick Change Inline sinker. These leger weights should be heavy enough to sink the float if it's set under depth so that they can help you plumb the depth.**
- **E-S-P Power Gum. An alternative to the braid stops and a neat replacement if the braid stop is cut by the line and must be replaced. Tying a Power Gum stop knot avoids you having to re-tackle the entire rig.**
- **Two large-bore beads. They act as a buffer between the float and the leger and the braid stops setting the depth of the rig.**
- **The wire trace you've just learned to tie and which will have been unloaded from a rig bin.**

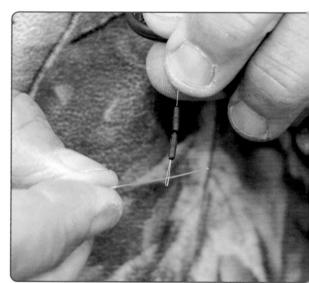

2 Thread the 15lb mainline through the wire loop housing the braid stops.

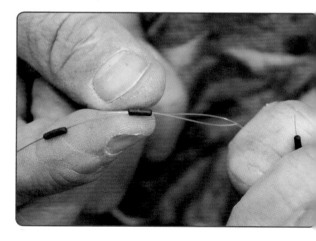

3 Slide two braid stops off the wire and on to the nylon line.

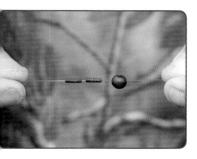

4 Add a hard large-bore bead on to the line.

5 Thread on the float followed by a large, soft rubber bead.

6 Then add the large sinker weight – remember that it must be able to sink the float.

7 Tie on the wire trace and slide the sinker down to the swivel.

8 Push the weight over the round eye to lock it to the swivel. This makes the rig more stable for casting.

9 The finished rig ready to be baited and cast out. To use it properly set the rig under the depth of the water and cast it out – the sinker should pull the float under. Bring the rig in, slide the braid stops up the line and re-cast. Keep repeating this process until the float tip pokes above the water to indicate that the rig is set 'dead depth'. Finally, slide the stops another 12–18in (30–45cm) over-depth and you're ready to bait the rig and get fishing!

10 When you cast out tighten up to the float until about two-thirds of the blaze tip is standing proud of the water. Keep your eyes locked on the float and wait for it to move!

187

Mounting deadbaits and a long-range leger rig

Using dead fish to tempt pike is probably the easiest way to catch them. Many different types can be used but it's probably the case that sea fish are now the most commonly used variety of deadbait, with mackerel, smelt, herring and sprats the favourite choices.

As anyone who visits a fishmonger knows, sea fish have very strong and distinct smells, and many types of bait – particularly mackerel – leak natural oils into the water that pike find very attractive.

While pike may be very efficient hunters of live fish they're also opportunists that are not adverse to scavenging on dead fish. Here's how you mount a typical deadbait on the wire trace we've shown you how to tie:

Above: Smelt, mackerel, lamprey, sardine, roach and herring are great pike deadbaits that will all catch predators.

1 The top treble nearest to the swivel is the load-bearing hook for casting. Sink this into the root of the tail on the deadbait; it's the toughest part of the fish that gives the tightest grip. Use the barbed hook for extra purchase.

2 The treble hook on the end of the trace is now lightly slipped into the flank at the bottom of the deadbait. Again use the barbed point to secure the hook. Don't bury the hook – lightly nicking the bait gives better hooking performance when a pike picks up your hookbait.

3 Here's the finished half mackerel hookbait ready to be cast out. It pays to use bait as fresh as you can get it, as it leaks nice oils into the water to tempt pike into feeding.

4 While tail sections are normally used fish heads can also do the job, as this shot shows. Here's a pike that couldn't resist a mackerel head.

Casting the distance

The float rig we've shown you is excellent for fishing lakes, reservoirs, canals and even slow-moving rivers where you might have to go over-depth by an extra foot or so.

Fishable at distances up to 50yd (45m) or so with a powerful rod, if you need to cast further you may need to change to a straight leger rig where the float is removed to reduce resistance and increase casting range.

Here's how Mick ties and uses his leger rig…

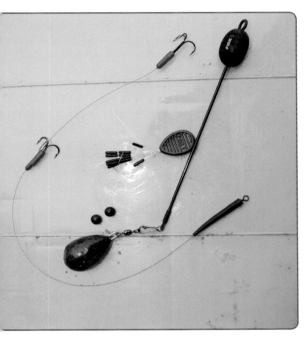

1 Here's the kit you need to tie the rig (above):

- Fox Braid Stops.
- Two large-bore beads.
- A 2–4oz leger weight.
- A Fox Predator Leger Stem.
- Your wire trace.

3 Tighten up the line between rod and leger. Lay the rod on two rod rests and position the spool of the reel directly over the top of a drop-off swing arm bite indicator.

2 Thread two braid stops then the beads and the leger stem on to the mainline. Tie the wire trace on to nylon line. Bait the hooks and cast out.

4 Slide the mainline into the clip on the bite indicator and ensure the line is held tight to the reel so that the drop-off indicator is held tight to the base of the spool. If a pike runs with the bait the line pulls out of the clip and the indicator clatters

back; if it picks up the bait and moves towards the bank the arm slowly falls. In both cases strike…fish on!

Looking after your pike

They're deadly, they look prehistoric and they're one of the most fearsome looking of fish – it's strange, then, that they're so delicate and need to be handled carefully and with great technique. Poor handling of a hooked pike can damage it, so we've put together a guide to landing, unhooking, weighing, photographing and returning your quarry safely.

Whatever you do, don't skimp on the kit you use for looking after pike on the bank: a good quality unhooking mat and tools that are made for dealing with treble hooks and wire traces will help you look after the fish you catch.

Here's Mick Rouse's guide to handling pike like a professional…

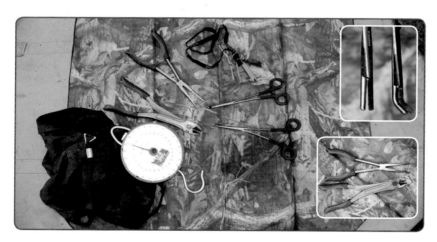

1 Here's the kit you'll need:

- A large, thick unhooking mat. Pike can flap when they're on the bank and need to be cushioned from the ground so that they don't damage themselves.
- Scales and a weigh sling. Ensure the scales are already zeroed to allow for quick weighing of your catch.
- 10–12in (25–30cm) straight and curved forceps. Different-shaped forceps are useful to reach awkwardly positioned hooks (inset above).
- 10–12in long-nosed pliers. They can help you gain extra purchase to remove deeply set hooks (inset above).
- Long-nosed cutters. If you can't remove a particularly awkwardly positioned hook cut the hook rather than tear it out – it's much safer for the fish.

2 When you land a pike carry it to the mat and straddle the fish with your knees. This gives you greater control over it and stops it flapping off the mat.

3 Ascertain where the hooks are and slide your fingers under the pike's gill cover on the opposite side to the hooks. DON'T grip the pink gill rakers – they should remain untouched at the back of your hand.

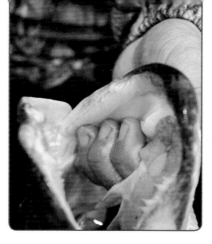

4 Apply gentle pressure with your fingers on the inside of the lower jaw. There's a natural gripping point where there are no teeth and it's safe for the angler (and the pike) to secure the fish with a firm grip.

5 Ease the fish's mouth open and clamp the forceps on to the top treble hook.

6 Turn your wrist over in the opposite direction to the bend of the hook to raise the top treble out of the pike. Lift clear of the fish's mouth to give better access to the second hook.

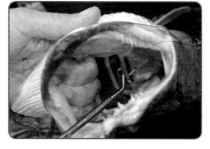

7 Clamp the forceps on to the lower treble and repeat the unhooking procedure.

8 Job done – the pike has been unhooked safely and is ready for weighing.

9 Quickly slide the fish into the wet weigh sling to record its weight.

10 To photograph the fish hold it firmly round the wrist of the tail with one hand and keep the gill-cover grip with your other hand. Take a couple of quick photos, carry the fish back to the water in the net or sling and release it as soon as its strength has returned.

11 Even taking all the care you can you'll still get the odd cut or graze off those mean teeth, so always carry a small plastic box packed with a first aid kit. Better safe than bleeding!

Glossary

Action – The bending of a rod when casting or playing a fish.

Bait rocket – Bait-loaded plastic tube with a buoyant nosecone that causes it to turn upside down when it hits the water; also known as a 'spod'.

Bankstick – Adjustable metal pole with a spike at the bottom for pushing into the ground and a thread at the top to which a rod rest can be screwed.

Big pit reel – Nickname for 10,000-size reels.

Bivvy – The small tent used by fishermen, usually when overnight fishing.

Boilie – Bait consisting of small balls of boiled dough usually made with eggs, milk protein powder and/or fishmeal, bird food. Flavours and colour can also be added.

Bolt rig – A rig that semi-fixes the leger weight on to the line, for the purpose of self-hooking the fish when it picks up the bait. This surprises the fish and makes it 'bolt'.

Braid blades – Strong scissors used to cut braided line.

Carp rod – Strong, powerful rod used in fishing for large, hard-fighting fish such as carp and tench.

Choppy – Chopped worms used as bait.

Chubber – Light, extra-buoyant float made of balsa or plastic; also called a 'loafer'.

Clutch – Tensioning device fitted in a reel to control how line is released when pulled from a reel by a hooked fish; also called the 'drag'.

Crashing – The leaping and rolling of carp near the surface.

Dead depth – The exact depth of the water.

Dotting down – Extent to which a float is submerged in the water.

Drag – Tensioning device fitted in a reel; also called the 'clutch'.

Drop-back bite – A bite in which the fish picks up the bait and swims back towards the angler, causing the line to go slack.

Droppers – Small shot spread through the lower half of a fishing line, intended to ensure a smooth drop or fall of the hookbait through the final part of its descent when cast.

Dust shot – Very small split shot.

Fast-taper action – The action of a rod in which the butt section is much stiffer than the tip in order to facilitate long-range casting.

Feathering the line – Dabbing your finger on the mainline pouring off the reel when a cast is made, to slow the final stage of its flight.

Feeder – Abbreviation of 'swimfeeder'.

Fizzing – Patch of small bubbles on the surface, a telltale sign of fish feeding on the bottom immediately below.

Freebies or **free offerings** – Food scattered as a lure in the area being fished; also referred to as 'loosefeed'.

Glugs – Nickname for flavoured solutions poured on boilies.

Groundbait – Bait thrown into the water to attract fish to the area.

Guides – The rings on a rod through which the line runs; also known as 'rod rings'.

Guzunder – A bite in which the float is pulled beneath the surface.

Hair rig – Set-up in which the bait is not attached directly to the hook but instead hangs from a short length of line just below it.

Hooklink or **hooklength** – The short length of line at the bottom of a float rig carrying the hook; also known as a 'hook-to-nylon', 'trace' or 'tail'. It is usually slightly weaker than the mainline.

Lead clip rig – Leger rig from which the weight can be jettisoned in an emergency.

Leger – A weight attached to the mainline to give it adequate casting weight; commonly called a lead.

Lift bite – A bite in which the float lifts slightly when a fish picks up some of the shot attached to the line.

Line bites – Twitches and pulls on the line caused by large fish bumping into it.

Loafer – Light, extra-buoyant float made of balsa or plastic; also called a 'chubber'.

Loosefeed – Food scattered as a lure in the area being fished; also referred to as 'freebies' or 'free offerings'.

Mainline – An alternative name for reel line.

Match rod – Responsive, lightweight rod of a type historically used in competition angling.

Mending the line – Flicking the line tight behind the float when fishing a river.

On-the-drop – Term used to describe bait being taken as it slowly sinks through the water.

Peg – The part of the water that you've decided to fish; also called a 'swim'.

Plumbing – Measuring the depth of the water.

Pole cup – Bait-filled cup attached to a special end section of a pole that can be upended at the point being fished.

Pole pot – Small variety of pole cup that's attached to the top bit of your pole.

Quivertip – The superfine and responsive top section of a rod used for legering and swimfeeder fishing.

Rig – The assembled tackle attached to the end of the line that's cast into the water.

Rod pod – A stand-alone frame that can hold two or three rods complete with bite alarms and rod rests.

Rod rings – The rings on a rod through which the line runs; also known as 'guides'.

Shelf-life baits – Boilies that have been treated with a preservative to stop them going mouldy.

Specimen fish – An imprecise term for a 'big fish' that varies across species and venues. For example, on some lakes a 20-pounder may be small, but on most venues it would rank as a specimen!

Spod – Bait-loaded plastic tube with a buoyant nosecone that causes it to turn upside down when it hits the water; also known as a 'bait rocket'.

Spodding – Fishing with a spod.

Strike – Angler's reaction to a bite on the line – the 'swish' of the rod to make the connection between fish and hook.

Swim – The part of the water that you've decided to fish; also called a 'peg'.

Swimfeeder – Heavy tube or cage attached to the line carrying additional bait to lure fish.

Tail – The short length of line at the bottom of a float rig carrying the hook; also known as a 'hooklink', 'hooklength', 'hook-to-nylon' or 'trace'.

Test curve rating or **TC** – Measurement of the weight that's needed to bend the tip of rod through 90°.

Trace – A special hooklink made out of wire and used in pike fishing.

Trotting – Running a float downriver without it being sucked under by the current.

Waggler – A float with only its bottom end attached to the line.